Discussion and Interaction
in the Academic Community

Discussion and Interaction in the Academic Community

Carolyn G. Madden and
Theresa N. Rohlck

 MICHIGAN SERIES IN ENGLISH FOR
ACADEMIC & PROFESSIONAL PURPOSES

Series Editors

Carolyn G. Madden and John M. Swales

Ann Arbor

THE UNIVERSITY OF MICHIGAN PRESS

Copyright © by the University of Michigan 1997
All rights reserved
ISBN 0-472-08290-6
Library of Congress Catalog Card No. 96-60544
Published in the United States of America by
The University of Michigan Press
Manufactured in the United States of America

2000   1999   1998   4   3   2

Preface

Much has taken place in the field of English as a second language to enable such a text as *Discussion and Interaction in the Academic Community* to be published. Particularly, the field has moved toward a goal of providing English for specific purposes to numerous students in the United States and in the international community. This text is a response to the specific needs of teaching and learning the skills, strategies, and discourse of academic oral communication. The text began as a course pack for a ten-week course at the English Language Institute at the University of Michigan. With the help and contributions of our students and colleagues, this text has grown and developed into the current volume.

We would particularly like to thank the many colleagues who have taught this course and to recognize those who have provided encouragement and comments and even directly contributed to the development of these materials. Among them are Elizabeth Axelson, Sarah Briggs, Margo Czinski, Risa Dean, Barbara Dobson, Christine Feak, Brenda Imber, Susan Reinhart, and Virginia Samuda. For administrative assistance in the early stages of the book we thank Cynthia Hudgins, and for assisting with the tedious task of getting copyright permissions we thank Liz Tompkins. Eric Ström offered assistance with photographs, for which we are especially grateful. We are indebted to the thoughtful comments of our reviewers and our ESL editor, Mary Erwin, and to the English Language Institute for providing funding for release time for this project. We also thank John Swales, Director of the ELI and coeditor of the series, who has offered intellectual and moral support throughout this project.

On a personal note, Theresa would like to thank Bob Oprandy for introducing her to the idea of materials development in the first place. She is also grateful to her family—Ayi, Antonio, and Mario—for their patience and for helping to keep things in perspective. Carolyn is grateful for the unconditional love of her father, Eugene J. Gleim.

Acknowledgments

Grateful acknowledgment is given to the following for use of copyrighted or manuscript material, and for permission to reprint previously published material.

American Journal of Economics and Sociology for table 1, p. 461, and tables 3 and 4, p. 463, from "An Analysis of Authors and Institutions Contributing to the AJES, 1981–93" by Mostafa Mehdizadeh, *American Journal of Economics and Sociology* vol. 52, no. 4 (October 1993): 459–66. Reprinted with permission.

American Sociological Association for graph, p. 340, and table, p. 341, from "Housework in Marital and Non-marital Households" by Scott J. South and Glenna Spitze, *American Sociological Review* vol. 59, no. 3 (June 1994): 327–47. Reprinted with permission of the authors.

Associated Press for "Ozone-Destroyer Declining, Study Says" by Paul Recer, *Ann Arbor News,* July 15, 1995, and "Graduate Exam Joining Computer Age," *Ann Arbor News,* November 15, 1993. Reprinted with permission.

Chronicle of Higher Education for "Foreign Influx in Science Found to Cut Americans' Participation" by Amy Magaro Rubin, *Chronicle of Higher Education,* and for "Labor Department Urged to Reconsider Policy That Raises Pay of Non-U.S. Researchers" by Amy Magaro Rubin, *Chronicle of Higher Education,* July 14, 1995, p. A33. Copyright ©1995. *Chronicle of Higher Education.* Reprinted with permission.

Educational Institute of the American Hotel & Motel Association for chart, p. 47, from *Managing Front Office Operations* by Charles E. Steadmore and Michael L. Kasavana (East Lansing, MI: Educational Institute of the American Hotel & Motel Association, 1988). Reprinted with permission.

Keiko Hirokawa, for transcripts from her Ph.D. dissertation, "Expressions of Culture in Conversational Styles of Japanese and Americans," University of Michigan (1995).

Newsweek for graph in "Chips Off the Block," *Newsweek,* February 20, 1995 (source: Blockbuster).

Scientific American for illustration by Lisa Burnett, p. 42 in "Population, Poverty and the Local Environment" by Partha S. Dasgupta, *Scientific American,* February 1995, 40–45. Copyright ©1995 by Scientific American, Inc. All rights reserved. Illustration by Johnny Johnson and Steven Stankiewicz, p. 52 in "The Aluminum

viii   **Acknowledgments**

Beverage Can" by William F. Hosford and John L. Duncan, *Scientific American,* September 1994, 48–53. Copyright ©1994 by Scientific American, Inc. All rights reserved.

Witoon Tirasophon for transcripts of his discussion on "Brain Drain."

United Press Syndicate for "The Far Side" cartoon by Gary Larson. The Far Side © Farworks, Inc./Dist. by Universal Press Syndicate. Reprinted with permission. All rights reserved.

U.S. Bureau of the Census for graph, p. 652 of *Statistical Abstract of the United States: 1995,* 115th ed. (Washington, D.C.: U.S. GPO, 1995).

Ellen Yu Wu for transcripts of her data presentation of the graph "Index of Consumer Sentiment and Car Sales."

Every effort has been made to trace the ownership of all copyrighted material in this book and to obtain permission for its use.

Contents

Unit 3. Presenting Data in the Academic Community   81

Appendixes   119

Introduction

Rationale

The increased focus on internationalism in business and academics has caused an increase in the awareness of the importance of interactive skills for both native and nonnative speakers (NNS). Recent statistics suggest that the influx of international students to the United States will continue to increase, and with that comes the need to provide effective language instruction relevant to the situation and needs of this community of students.

One of the primary focuses of this text is to enhance the ability of the NNS to contribute to the development of their disciplines and to the internationalism of the academic community. For many of the students one of the most difficult tasks is to interact effectively and confidently within the discussions, seminars, and ongoing dialogues in their disciplines. Students are often at a loss linguistically to make themselves heard and understood, much less to be able to inspire and enrich others. All of these tasks require opportunity, awareness, an understanding of communication strategies, knowledge of effective discourse, and a willingness to participate.

Objectives of the Text

Discussion and Interaction in the Academic Community (DI) is divided into three major sections. Unit 1 focuses on the student as a member of the academic community. The objective of the activities in this unit is to make students comfortable in this context, develop mutual respect, and provide a forum for developing awareness of group dynamics. Unit 2 focuses on the student as facilitator. The objective of the activities in this unit is to provide students with the opportunity to learn the skills, strategies, and discourse needed for effective seminar and discussion participation. Unit 3 focuses on the student as expert. The objective of the activities in this unit is to provide opportunities for students to present, critique, monitor, and improve upon the exchange of technical information.

The text builds on the expertise and the linguistic abilities of the learners. It assumes that, while many of the learners have a sense of their academic goals and have much information to bring to bear on any task, their ability to make their knowledge and objectives explicit in English is limited.

Audience

While the text was originally designed to meet the needs of graduate students in an English-speaking academic environment, who have a fairly defined sense of their research areas, the text also provides a reasonable framework for undergraduates as well. The activities are easily adaptable to a population such as the undergraduates who are perhaps not yet experts in their discipline.

The text would also be beneficial and appropriate for academic students in an English as a foreign language situation whose growth and development in the academic community is dependent on some experience with both the discourse and culture of the English-speaking academic community. It would be a particularly relevant text for developing programs within a university context abroad where the goal is to provide students with the skills and ability to participate in exchanges, discussions, and seminars in academic English.

Instructor's Role

As with every text in our series we are attempting to provide space for individual authorship of materials dependent on particular class needs and to give an opportunity for the students' personal and cultural voices to be represented. The experienced instructor will have significant opportunities to contribute text and activities to meet the needs of particular populations. For example, in the third unit there are materials from specific disciplines that are challenging but accessible to most students in varying fields in terms of the discourse and lexical demands. These offer a shared context for students to evaluate and negotiate how to improve the effectiveness of presenting and responding to an audience. It is particularly important, however, for the instructor and students to then bring to class their own texts and integrate the ethnography of their own discipline with the skills and strategies developed from the context of the course.

The accompanying instructor's notes and commentary provide suggestions and guidance for those who are perhaps new to the field of

English for Academic Purposes (EAP) or who have not yet had much experience building on the strong academic knowledge of this population.

Structure

DI offers a set of tasks that will set the pace and framework for an EAP course in oral communication. Each of the three units is divided into several lessons. Each lesson focuses on an aspect of functional or technical discourse related to the activities of international students in an academic context, such as participation in seminar discussions, the exchange of technical information, and consultations and interactions with peers and advisors. Each lesson may also include relevant idiomatic expressions, examples of actual student discourse, a fluency focus, taping activities, and options for homework. While the lessons are ordered intentionally, the activities need not always be used in order of presentation. For example, "Being Explicit: Giving Directions" in unit 3 may very well be used prior to students leading their own discussions. And while the climax of the text is in unit 2 with its emphasis on leading and participating in a discussion, it may be more advantageous for certain academic populations to focus on the technical information of unit 3 prior to unit 2. The appendixes include key aspects of certain tasks that need to be assigned by the instructor. This volume will provide materials for approximately twenty to forty hours of classwork depending on class size and the curriculum goals of a program.

Unit 1

Interacting in the Academic Community

Photo by Eric Ström

In this unit, you will focus on interacting as a member of the academic community. The objective of the activities in this unit is to make you comfortable in this context, to help you and your peers develop mutual respect, and to provide a forum for developing awareness of the dynamics of interaction with peers and faculty in the context of a university setting. Many of the activities will require you to interview a native English speaker in order to give you an opportunity to interact and to help you gather some interesting information about your community. A few of the activities, such as "Getting to Know You" and "Small Talk," are meant to provide you with an opportunity to feel comfortable with your classmates; some of the other activities, such as "Excuses and Messages," will give you practice in preparing for your interactions with your professors and advisors.

1

Student Information Questionnaire

Name _____   Telephone _____

                                       E-mail _____

❑ Undergrad   ❑ Grad   ❑ Staff   ❑ Visitor

Country _____   Language(s) _____

Field of Study/Area of Research _____

How long have you been in the United States? _____

In your opinion, what are your strongest skills in English?
(reading/writing/understanding/interacting/presenting/pronunciation)

_____

In your opinion, what are your weakest language skills?

_____

What would you like to study/learn in this course? Check as many as you
want.   *p. 47*
   ❑   giving and getting opinions
   ❑   idioms
   ❑   summarizing/paraphrasing skills
   ❑   interrupting strategies
   ❑   feedback strategies
   ❑   discussion skills
   ❑   other (list)

      _____

      _____

Have you had an opportunity to participate in any of the following?

In English   In your native language
   ❑   seminar/discussion   ❑   seminar/discussion
   ❑   academic advising or   ❑   academic advising or
       consultation sessions   consultation sessions
   ❑   interview   ❑   interview
   ❑   presentation   ❑   presentation

Getting to Know You

For this activity, you will be divided into two groups (A and B). In the top right corner of the diagram below, circle the letter of the group you are assigned to. In appendix 1 there are two sets of questions. If you are in group A, answer the questions on the page marked Group A, and if you are in group B, answer the questions on the page marked Group B. You will need to fill in the diagram below with your answers. After you are finished, your instructor will pair you with a student from the other group. Then you will compare your answers and questions and discuss any differences.

A B

1. _____

2. _____

3. _____

4. _____

5. _____

6. _____

Small Talk

For this activity you will need to get up and move around the room, as if you were at a party and had to mingle with the crowd. If you are not sure of what to say, you might find that asking a question is a good strategy to get yourself involved in conversation.

- Ask your classmates the following questions to find out some information about them.
- Ask a "follow-up" question to find out more details. The questions below each number (i.e., which one, what kind, where, how, etc.) give you hints for some of the follow-up questions, but you may also come up with your own.
- Don't ask all of the questions of one person; you should talk to everyone in the room.

Find someone who

1. plays a musical instrument   _____

    (which instrument?)   _____

2. has studied martial arts   _____

    (what kind, how long?)   _____

3. owns a car   _____

    (what kind?)   _____

4. is studying engineering   _____

5. is a transfer student   _____

    (from which school?)   _____

6. likes to cook   _____

    (what kind of food?)   _____

7. was born in the United States   _____

    (where?)   _____

8. likes American pizza   _____

      (what kind?)   _____

9. is married   _____

      (for how long?)   _____

10. speaks more than two languages   _____

      (which ones?)   _____

11. likes to play or watch soccer   _____

12.   _____

13.   _____

14.   _____

Let's Talk

Clearly the word "talk" can be used in two totally different senses. On the one hand, it can mean simply "to utter words," as in "Archibald's got a talking parrot which says *Damn* if you poke it." On the other hand, it can mean "to use language in a meaningful way."

—R. Wardhaugh, in *Investigating Language*

The following words all have something to do with talking. Match the words with the appropriate sentence. Discuss your answers with your partner(s).

comment	discuss	talk
converse	mention	mumble

1. When you see Elaine, would you please _mention_ to her that I have her lab book?

2. If you want people to listen to you, don't _mumble_.

3. Unfortunately we have run out of time; perhaps next week we can _converse_ about this during office hours.

4. At the meeting on Thursday, they will _discuss_ next year's contract for the teaching assistants.

5. Carl wanted to be able to _converse_ with his friends in Portuguese, as well as in English.

6. The professor didn't _comment_ on the international student's English; she paid attention only to the content of the paper.

facilitate	present	address	negotiate
interrupt	lecture	interview	give feedback

The above words describe different ways we communicate and are frequently used in academic contexts. Which words fit the following situations? The italicized words are clues.

7. Your job in your group is to *talk to the others* and *help* the activity move along smoothly.

   facilitate

8. You and your group are all *talking together to resolve a problem.*

   negotiating

9. You *talk* to some American students and *ask them questions.*

   interviewing

10. Someone else is *giving information to the whole class*

    lecturing

    and you have something to say, so *you start talking at the same time.*

    interrupting

11. Your *teacher is talking to a group*

    presenting

    and some of the people in the audience are *telling her something by*

    nodding their heads.

    giving feedback

12. The president of the university is going *to speak to all of the students*

    at the graduation ceremony.

    address

Greetings and Responses

There are a variety of greetings and responses used in American English. Which ones you use will often depend on *the context and the people involved.* Some greetings and responses in English are "formulaic." Are there similar phrases in your own language?

Below are several greetings with some possible responses listed. With your partner, decide which responses are appropriate for the situation. There may be more than one appropriate response for each greeting.

1. *Friend:* How's it going?
    You: a. I'm off to lunch.
                b. Fine, thanks.
                c. Great!

2. *Professor:* Hello Carlos, how are you?
    You: a. Fine, thank you, and you?
                  b. Not bad.
                  c. OK.

3. *You:*   Hi, Alex, what's new?
    Your roommate: a. Oh, nothing much.
                      b. Fine, thanks.
                      c. Nothing.

See if you can also label the speakers in the following situations.

4. _____: Where are you off to?

    _____: a. Just doing some errands.
                    b. Oh, nothing much.
                    c. Going to the post office. Need anything?

5. _____: What's up?

    _____: a. OK.
                    b. Oh, nothing much.
                    c. Fine, and you?

What are some other greetings and responses you have heard or used? Try them out with your partner and write them in the spaces below.

_____

_____

_____

The Culture of the Campus

Interview an American student and find out the following.

Name (first only is OK) _____

Major/Field of study _____

Hometown and state _____

How long in this city _____

Do you like studying here? Why/why not?

_____

_____

Do you like living in this city? Why/why not?

_____

_____

Two good restaurants _____

A restaurant to avoid and why _____

A good place to buy books _____

A good place to buy music (cassettes/CDs) _____

Two enjoyable things to do on the weekend _____

_____

A useful piece of advice for newcomers to the university and the city

_____

_____

[this page may be reproduced as needed]

Colloquial Challenges

What's appropriate? Some phrases are difficult to understand because of their colloquial usage and because they are usually used in certain contexts. For example, you wouldn't say to your professor, "Come on, you're crazy!" but you might say it to a good friend who has just told you she's going to quit college in order to work in a factory. With your partner, read the following conversations and answer the questions.

Conversation 1

A: **Come on** guys, we need to finish this report tonight.
B: Why? I thought we had 'til Friday.
A: No way, he said he'd take off points if we waited 'til Friday.
B: Oh, **come on,** I don't think he will.
C: _____

1. Who is talking?
2. Who is "he" in line 3?
3. What are some possibilities for the next line in the conversation?
4. Can you find another colloquialism that suggests disagreement with a friend?

Conversation 2

D: I'm afraid there's little I can do about your grade. This article seems to be very professional but there are no citations.
E: **I don't follow.** Is it good or not very good? **What are you getting at? Are you suggesting** _____ ?

5. Who's talking? What's going on?
6. How does "E" feel?
7. What is "D" suggesting? How might you complete the conversation?

These phrases can be used to express disbelief, anger, or impatience when there is confusion.	These phrases are more neutral, that is, less confrontational.
What are you getting at? What are you suggesting?	I don't quite understand. I don't follow. Could you explain what you mean?

Rapport and Complaining

What's there to complain about around the university, in class, in your department? Why do we complain? Surprisingly, two recent authors, Boxer and Pickering (1995), have suggested that complaining is a way to make friends, that is, to build rapport with your classmates and colleagues at a university. Read the following interaction, taken from Boxer and Pickering's article. "A" and "B" are two female graduate students in a departmental library.

> *A:* They never have what you need in here. You'd think they'd at least have the important books and articles.
> *B:* They didn't have what you were looking for?
> *A:* No.
> *B:* That's typical.

"A" is complaining. Does "B" agree with "A"? Does "B" feel the same way as "A" does about the library?

Now read the next example and choose one of the three responses that you think would help build rapport.

1. A classmate mentions to you at the end of class that the professor is just giving too many assignments.

    > *A:* Can you believe how many assignments we have—and this is only the second week of class!

    Your response is:
    - ❏ How many?
    - ❏ I don't think so.
    - ❏ I know, it seems like a lot.

How would you show that you support or are sympathetic with the speaker in the following situations? Complete the dialogues in the following scenarios. Use the exchanges given above as examples.

2. A classmate is wondering if the microeconomics instructor is ever going to give some good examples to illustrate the concepts.

    > *A:* You'd think he could just give us some good *examples* to make these concepts clearer.

You:

A:

You:

3. Your professor is having a difficult time getting her paper finished for a conference because of all the students she has to see.

> *Professor:* Seems like I've seen *everyone* from class the last couple of days—and just when I've been trying to finish up this paper for the conference next week.
>
> *You:*
>
> *Professor:*
>
> *You:*

You can't (or might not *want* to) always show support. Perhaps there are issues that you'd rather not comment on. What do you think about the following situations? Would you be able to show support in these situations or not?

- A classmate starts complaining about the lecturing style of a professor you think is brilliant.
- The secretary in your department tells you the department chair is difficult to work for.
- A classmate has trouble understanding the international teaching assistant in the biology lab.
- Your TA starts complaining about the papers he has to correct.

With your partner(s), each of you choose at least two of the following services or issues at your university/school. Spend about one to two minutes discussing any complaints you have about each one. Show support for each other's viewpoint where possible.

housing

transportation

food

tuition

Simulation

teaching

about

computer services

Complaint

research opportunities

advisor availability

other services or issues _____

do homework

Academic Life Survey No. 1

Arranging your academic life at a U.S. university is often a challenge. There are a lot of people and resources available to you as a student to help you with this task—for example, your professor or teaching assistant, your academic advisor, even your friends and colleagues.

- First do the survey below with a classmate.
- *no* • Then, for homework, find two students, one American and one international, and complete the survey on the next page.
- Remember *you* must *ask* the questions.

Person surveyed	Survey completed by
Name:	Name:
Field/Dept.:	Date:
Year of Study:	
Native Country:	

1. a. Have you ever visited a professor during his/her office hours?
        yes ❑   no ❑
    b. Have you ever visited a TA during his/her office hours?
        yes ❑   no ❑

2. How often do you meet your academic advisor?
        once a week ❑   once a year ❑
        once a month ❑   never have ❑

3. Besides your academic advisor, who else do you talk to for academic advice?
        no one else ❑   the department secretary ❑
        other students ❑   other professors ❑
        friends ❑   other ❑

4. Does your academic schedule leave you any free time?
        yes ❑   if yes, what do you do in your free time? _____
        no ❑   if no, what would you like to do in your free time? _____

5. Where do you most often study?
        at the library ❑   at your office ❑
        at home, apartment, or dorm ❑   never study ❑
        at your friend's house ❑   other place ❑

Academic Life Survey No. 1: Homework

Person surveyed   Survey completed by
Name: Name:
Field/Dept.:   Date:
Year of Study:
Native Country:

1. a. Have you ever visited a professor during his/her office hours?
        yes ❏   no ❏
    b. Have you ever visited a TA during his/her office hours?
        yes ❏   no ❏

2. How often do you meet your academic advisor?
        once a week ❏   once a year ❏
        once a month ❏   never have ❏

3. Besides your academic advisor, who else do you talk to for academic advice?
        no one else ❏   the department secretary ❏
        other students ❏   other professors ❏
        friends ❏   other ❏

4. Does your academic schedule leave you any free time?
        yes ❏   if yes, what do you do in your free time? _____
        no ❏   if no, what would you like to do in your free time? _____

5. Where do you most often study?
        at the library ❏   at your office ❏
        at home, apartment, or dorm ❏   never study ❏
        at your friend's house ❏   other place ❏

[this page may be reproduced as needed]

Excuses and Messages   *Simulations*   *Impromptu*

Read the following episodes and decide what you would do. Are there any differences between these situations in the United States and similar situations in your country?

1. You want to make an appointment with your advisor. You haven't been able to reach her by phone so you will try to E-mail her. Write the message to your advisor.

    ```
    Date:
    From:
    To:
    Subject:
    ```

2. You're late for an appointment with your advisor. When you arrive at her office you find that she is not there.

    What would you do?   ❏ just leave
                          ❏ try to find someone (i.e., a secretary or administrator) and try to explain to him/her why you are late
                          ❏ leave a note

Write a note to your advisor.

3. You missed a class because you couldn't get the assignment completed on time.

    What would you do?   ❏ go to the next class with the assignment and say nothing
    ❏ go to the next class and explain why the assignment was late
    ❏ E-mail the instructor and explain

    Write an E-mail message explaining your absence and the late assignment.

    ```
    Date:
    From:
    To:
    Subject:
    ```

4. You go to your professor's office during his regular office hours and he is not there. You have something important to find out about your assignment.

    What would you do?   ❏ find a secretary and see if you can find out when he will be in his office
    ❏ leave your number with a note in his mailbox
    ❏ phone his home

Write a note including your phone number for the professor. What kind of information do you need to include?

Negotiating the Office Hour

What are reasons for visiting your advisor? Recent research (McChesney 1994) cites four main reasons why students go to office hours to see their advisors.

- to seek information on courses
- to discuss completion of requirements
- to discuss projects and papers
- to receive waivers and exemptions

Can you think of any other reasons why you might go to your advisor?

Results of Academic Life Survey No. 1 usually show that international students go to their advisors less frequently than American students. Did the results of your survey support this?

Research by Bardovi-Harlig and Hartford (1993) suggests that when students go to their advisors to discuss/negotiate which courses they should take, certain strategies that the students use are more successful than others. Observations of taped advising sessions show that students often do one of the following things during the interaction.

- The student initiates a suggestion.
- The student has no suggestion.

Look at the following question an advisor ("A") asks a student during an advising session.

A: Now, what, what do you want to take in the, in the fall?

What sort of response do you think the advisor is expecting from the student?

Now look at four student ("S") responses to the question, taken from the Bardovi-Harlig and Hartford research, and answer the questions that follow.

a. S: Yes, uh . . . well I'm thinking of, oh, ah, Historical Linguistics.
b. S: In fact, uh, I'm not . . . used to these, uh, courses provided by this, eh, department, so I . . . I want to have, uh, advice from you.
c. S: Perhaps I should also mention that I have an interest in sociolinguistics and would like, if I can, to structure things in such a way that I might do as much sociolinguistics as I can.
d. S: Is it possible, um, possible to take L542. That is, phonological descriptions, this semester?

Can you tell what strategy the student is using in each example?

Which example is closest to what you think the advisor is expecting? Which is farthest from what is expected?

Which do you prefer? Which have you used/might you use?

Look at the following interactions. Which one appears more appropriate in talking with your advisor, "e" or "f"?

e. A: What were the other courses you were thinking of taking?
    S: Yeah, **I'm going to take,** ah . . . applied . . . transformation syntax.
f. A: What is it you were thinking about taking next fall?
    S: Um, there are two required courses. So I think **I need to take** for this semester . . . and . . .

What is the difference between **I'm going to take** and **I need to take?**

In the following, underline the phrases that might not be appropriate.

g. S: So, I, I just decided on taking the language structure . . . field method in linguistics.
h. S: In the summer I will take language testing for the first summer session, the first one, the second summer session I will take the socio [linguistics class].

Underline the phrases that make the following student comments appropriate.

i. S: I was thinking also the linguistic department, the uh historical issues, historical linguistics . . . I think you, you teach that.
j. S: Well, these are the courses I would like to take in the fall.

Homework

Find out if there are any prerequisites or other requirements that you must fulfill in your department for next semester and what courses you would like to take next semester. Is there any conflict between what you need to take and what you want to take?

Requirements for next semester

_____

_____

_____

Courses interested in taking next semester

_____

_____

_____

Be prepared to take turns with your partner in role-playing an advisor-student interaction, using the information you gathered about your own course requirements.

Academic Life Survey No. 2

The academic world in the United States may be quite different from the academic world you came from. One difference might be in the relationship between students and professors or teaching assistants. In Academic Life Survey No. 1 you discovered some of those differences from a student's perspective. Here is a survey that will give you the professors' and/or teaching assistants' perspective.

- First, in class, ask your instructor the questions in the survey below.
- Then, for homework, find two professors and/or teaching assistants and complete the survey on the next page.

Person surveyed	Survey completed by
Name:	Name:
Professor or Teaching Assistant:	Date:
Field/Dept.:	

1. Do you expect students to visit you during your office hours?

    yes ❑   no ❑

2. Do you expect to see *all* of your students at least once per term?

    yes ❑   no ❑

3. Do you expect to see students only before exams?

    yes ❑   no ❑

4. What should students do if they cannot meet you during your office hours?

    make appointment ❑   call on phone ❑   other ❑ (specify)

    leave a note ❑   E-mail ❑   _____

5. Should students always make an appointment to see you, or should they just stop by during office hours?

    make appointment ❑   just stop by ❑

Optional: If there are a significant number of international students at your school, ask the following question.

6. Who do you see more frequently during office hours?

    native speakers ❑   nonnative speakers ❑

Academic Life Survey No. 2: Homework

Person surveyed   Survey completed by
Name: Name:
Professor or Teaching Assistant: Date:
Field/Dept.:

1. Do you expect students to visit you during your office hours?
    yes ❑   no ❑

2. Do you expect to see *all* of your students at least once per term?
    yes ❑   no ❑

3. Do you expect to see students only before exams?
    yes ❑   no ❑

4. What should students do if they cannot meet you during your office
    hours?
    make appointment ❑   call on phone ❑   other ❑ (specify)
    leave a note ❑   E-mail ❑   _____

5. Should students always make an appointment to see you, or should
    they just stop by during office hours?
    make appointment ❑   just stop by ❑

Optional: If there are a significant number of international students at
           your school, ask the following question.

6. Who do you see more frequently during office hours?
    native speakers ❑   nonnative speakers ❑

[this page may be reproduced as needed]

Active Listening 1

One side of interacting in the academic community involves taking a role as a speaker by asking questions, conducting interviews, taking part in conversations, even by complaining and making excuses. There is another side to interacting, that of listening. Successful interactions require your active participation as both a speaker and a listener.

This next activity will introduce you to Active Listening. First, answer the following questions and discuss with the class.

1. How do you let people know you are listening or paying attention to what they are saying?

2. How do you let people know you are confused or that you simply do not know what they've just said to you?

3. What are some examples of nonverbal feedback? Think about how this might vary from culture to culture. Give examples of nonverbal feedback in your culture.

4. How long do you wait before you interrupt or give feedback or ask a question? How does this differ from culture to culture?

The following transcripts are taken from *Expressions of Culture in Conversational Styles of Japanese and Americans* (Hirokawa 1995). The conversation about playing golf takes place between a native speaker of English (A) and a nonnative speaker (B). "A" begins by talking about how often he plays golf. The transcript has been slightly adapted for clarity.

Read the transcript of the conversation, then discuss the questions that follow.

   [1]*A:*   Oh, I maybe play uh once or twice a year

     B: ah

     A: and I've never shot less than 100 and a few weeks ago

     B: Mhm

   [5]*A:*   I went to San Francisco for spring break

B: Ah, yeah spring yeah San Francisco yeah is very good weather

A: Yeah you can golf everyday of the year
(nods)

B: Yeah, everyday not here
(nods)

A: Yeah

[10]*B:* Yeah

A: But my brother and I played a small

B: Mhmm

A: 9-hole course

B: Mhm
(nods)

[15]*A:* par 3

B: Mhm
(nods)

A: and I don't think we probably shot 49 or 50

B: (laughs)

A: Very embarrassing I mean short holes

[20]*B:* Mhm

A: but still we put the balls on the far side

B: Ah hah
(nods)

A: and would go into the woods

B: Yeah

[25]*A:* It's very embarrassing

B: yeah, I feel I uh have the same feeling

A: yeah
(nodding)

B: Yeah

Now, in your small group, discuss what indicates active listening in the above transcript.

5. Would you characterize "B" as a good listener? Why or why not?

6. Would you offer "B" any suggestions? Is there too much "good listening?"

7. Would you offer "A" any suggestions? Is there too little interaction?

Now take a look at the next transcript, also taken from *Expressions of Culture in Conversational Styles of Japanese and Americans* (Hirokawa 1995). This is a conversation between two native speakers (C and D) who are talking about working in Japan over the summer.

Read the transcript of the conversation, then discuss the questions that follow.

Key to markings on transcript:
    Pauses or silences indicated by . . .
    Overlap of speakers indicated by vertical line

[1]C: I . . . you know I've been I'm going to Japan this summer and um

 D: Mhm To study or
                                                                         (nods)

 C: To work   to work   I'm not sure if I'll be teaching English   or
                D: (nods)   D: (nods)   D: (nods)

 C: if I'll be getting a job with, I might be getting a job with Sumitomo

[5]D: (nods) I banked with Sumitomo (laughs)

 C: Really? Yeah they have like several companies including a bank and some
            D: (nods)   D: (nods)

 C: others (I'll be like) I think the work is with the trading company and I
          D: (nods)   D: (nods)

 C: forgot to say what I was gonna say . . . oh yeah they're um it's . . . oh yeah I did

      forget what I was going to say oh well (laughs)

¹⁰D: (Laughs) How'd you get the job?

   C: Um they've an office right across the hall from my dad's office

                                                    D: (nods)   D: (nods)

   C: and so I just called them up and you know introduced myself and he said,

                          D: (nods)

   C: "Oh, you're the kid whose father's" (smile)

   D: (nods and smiles) That's nice

¹⁵C: (Laughs) So that

   D: That always helps (laughs)

   C: Yeah (laughs) and then even right after that they were met he he he and his wife

      looked

   C: another company   another couple in their company went out with my dad

                   D: (nods)

   D: Mhm
     (nods)

²⁰C: to a restaurant in the Detroit area that the company runs

   D: Mhm
     (nods)

   C: and so I think my dad's pulling for me (smiles)

Now, in your small group discuss the following questions.

8. How would you describe the conversation between "C" and "D"? How does it differ from the conversation between "A" and "B" in the first transcript?

9. Find the question "D" asks and underline it. What is the function of this question in the conversation?

10. Underline the interruptions. Are they helpful or impolite?

Common Questions—Common Knowledge

In Class

With a partner, discuss the first three questions. Fill in your answers.

1. What questions are you asked most frequently by Americans?

2. What topics do you frequently hear being discussed on the bus, around town, etc.?

3. Since you have been here, what question(s) have you been asked that have surprised you?

Now, as a class, compare your responses.

Homework

Is your country frequently mentioned in U.S. news? What do you think Americans know about your country?

Interview at least two Americans and find out the following information. If the person you are interviewing answers yes to a question, ask them a follow-up question to keep the conversation going.

1. Do they know the leader of your country?   yes ❏   no ❏

                                                                yes ❏   no ❏

    comments: _____

2. Do they know where your country is located?   yes ❏   no ❏

                                                                yes ❏   no ❏

    comments: _____

3. Do they know anything about the history of your country?   yes ❏   no ❏

yes ❏   no ❏

comments: _____

4. Where are they most likely to hear or read international news?

TV ❏ (which channel?)   Radio ❏ (which station?)

Newspaper ❏ (which ones?)   Magazines ❏ (which ones?)

comments: _____

Listening to the News

Homework

Listen to a radio newscast or watch a television news report and complete the following information. You will use this information in an activity during the next class. You will need to retell one of the news items to a classmate, so make sure you have enough details written down so that you will be able to talk about it for a couple of minutes. You should take notes while you listen to the reports to help you remember the details.

1. What report did you listen to?
   What channel or station?
   Time?
   Date?

2. News reports may have several stories in each of the following categories. Choose one story for each category below and summarize.

   a. International or National News

   b. Local News

   c. Sports

   d. Weather

3. What story was delivered first? Why?

4. In what ways was this news report similar to or different from the news reports in your country?

In Class

Briefly discuss questions 3 and 4 with the whole class.

Active Listening 2

The next activity will give you a chance to focus on your active listening skills.

Each group will have three participants—**Speaker, Active Listener, Observer.** The speaker will present the national or international news story from the homework assignment. If there is considerable overlap in news stories, you may choose to tell a short personal story instead. Here is what each person should do.

As the **Speaker,** you should

- let the Active Listener start the conversation
- tell your story to the Active Listener
- keep the conversation interactive
- give full answers to any questions

As the **Active Listener,** you should

- start the conversation
- keep the conversation going
- make sure you are following what the Speaker is talking about
- ask questions/interrupt if needed
- give verbal and nonverbal feedback to the Speaker

As the **Observer,** you should

- complete the tally sheet on the next page *during* the conversation
- give the Speaker and Active Listener feedback on their "performance"

Observer's Tally Sheet

Tally how many times the Active Listener did the following.

interrupted _____

asked a question _____

gave verbal feedback _____

gave nonverbal feedback _____

In your group, discuss the following questions.

1. Was the Active Listener an effective listener?

2. Discuss the kind of feedback the listener gave. Was it effective?

3. What strategies were most effective for both the Speaker and the Active Listener?

4. Who participated the most in this conversation, the Speaker or the Active Listener? Or were they equal participants?

Think about how actively *you* listen in class, group discussions, lectures, seminars. Is it different depending on the context?

[this page may be reproduced as needed]

Interruptions

Deciding when to interrupt a conversation can be difficult. Whether you want to ask for clarification about something or simply make a contribution to the conversation, getting the attention of the speaker may be a challenge. In the following activity, you will practice interrupting at least once during a short discussion.

- First, each of you will select a topic from the following list or come up with one of your own.
- Check with your partners to make sure that you each have chosen a different topic.
- Take a few minutes to prepare what you will say in a two minute impromptu presentation on the topic.

Possible topics are as follows.

impressions of Americans

studying in a foreign university

research expectations at your university

use of advanced technology in teaching

world politics

art and censorship

genetic engineering

economic system of your country

Each group will have three participants: a **Speaker,** a **Designated Interrupter,** and a **Listener.** You will each have a chance to play all three roles. Decide who will do what in the first round. The Designated Interrupter's instructions will differ from round to round, but they will always involve some sort of interruption. These instructions can be found in appendix 2.

As the **Speaker,** you should

- speak for 1–2 minutes on the topic you chose

As the **Designated Interrupter,** you should

- follow the instructions given by the instructor
- read these instructions before the speaker begins to be sure you understand what you should do

As the **Listener(s),** you should

- provide appropriate feedback to the Speaker

After one round, check to see how well you did. Was the interrupter successful in completing his/her task?

Reading the News

Some people prefer to read the news in newspapers or magazines instead of listening to reports on the radio or watching the TV news. Depending on where you live, your city might have one or two local papers in addition to the newspapers from the nearest big city. Many campuses have student newspapers that offer topics of particular interest and relevance to students. Often people will first skim through a paper and read the headlines of articles in order to decide if the article is worth reading.

With your partner, match the first part of these newspaper headlines (on the left) with the second part of the headline (on the right). Based on the completed headlines, which article(s) would you be most interested in reading?

Tuition Hike

Curriculum or Not,

Americans Want
Government

Shaping an
Affordable Future:

Japanese Investment in

First Woman to
Fly Shuttle

New Research Suggests

Mutual Fund Firms Try

Corporate Profits
Robust

Addressing the Cost
of Education

on a Mission

Virus May Cause
Kaposi's Sarcoma

Teachers Teach Values

Speaking in
Plain English

Good Day Care

Despite Slowing Growth

Lowest in Years

to Keep Children
from Smoking

Homework

Look through a newspaper or news magazine. Find an article on a
controversial topic or on a topic that you have an opinion about. Read the
article and be prepared to tell about what you have read. You will use this
article to get you started on giving and getting opinions in the next unit.

Idioms in the News

Whether you are a baseball fan or not, you will probably run across some of these very common idiomatic expressions that use terms from the American sport of baseball. As you can see from the next page, these idioms frequently show up in the news and are often used when talking about politics. However it is not uncommon to hear them used in academic contexts as well.

If you are familiar with baseball, you might be able to guess the meaning of these phrases from the context and from your knowledge of the game. Work with a partner to figure out what the italicized phrases mean. What is another way to express the thought?

The president will have to start *playing hardball* soon if he expects to get his economic plan working.

The vice president seemed well prepared at the press conference until one reporter *threw him a curve.*

I don't think John was listening very well because his question about economic trends during class was just *out of left field.*

Since the ambassador was out of the country his assistant had to *pinch hit* for him and give the welcoming speech at the embassy.

I can't afford to *strike out* with my presentation this afternoon. I really need to do well but I'm so nervous.

The city council member *hit a home run* with her proposal for a new park in the center of town.

Are there other idiomatic phrases from baseball or other sports that you've heard or read? What context were they used in?

THE FAR SIDE   By GARY LARSON

"And then wham! This thing just came
right out of left field."

Playing Hardball

Clinton's triple play of issues may strike out with the public

Brenda Marshall may have a hit first time at bat

Participating in the
Academic Community

Photo by Eric Ström

In this unit you will focus on being an active participant in the academic
community. The objective of the activities in this unit is to provide you with
the opportunity to learn the skills, strategies, and discourse needed for
effective seminar and discussion participation. Many of the activities
engage you in giving and getting opinions, formulating effective questions,
and summarizing. This engagement provides you with a chance to discover
and develop your repertoire of effective phrases in organizing, leading, and
participating in a discussion. The activities mostly emanate from current
readings of general interest to an academic community. The feedback
sessions give you a chance to monitor your development and to critique the
skills and language of your peers.

Opinions and Discussions: Getting Started

You have each brought to class the article in the news about a topic or issue that is controversial to discuss with your group (homework from p. 41).

- First, choose a facilitator, someone who will make sure the task gets accomplished.
- Decide who will go first, second, etc., in each group.
- Have the first person present the news item and ask the others about their opinions of the issue/topic.
- Talk about each item for 3–5 minutes.

Here are some useful phrases to begin with.

What do you think about . . . ?

How do you feel about . . . ?

Do you agree with . . . ?

Are you opposed to . . . ?

What is your country's position on . . . ?

Did you find it difficult to give your opinion or ask for an opinion? Were you able to ask for clarification? How do you show that you are not sure? How do you challenge someone's views? In the following activities, you will learn how to do these things. You will find that having the language to express your views will be useful to you not only in this class, but in your other academic classes, and in your life outside of the academic environment.

Giving and Getting Opinions

Below are some of the ways we ask for and give our opinions. These phrases will be useful as part of your discussion task.

- What phrases can you add to each category below?
- In what contexts are some phrases not appropriate?
- Try some of them with different intonation and see how the meaning changes.

Asking for an Opinion

Which of these is trying to get you to agree?

   What do you think/feel about . . . ?

   Would you agree/say that . . . ?

   Jae Hoon, what's your opinion on/about . . . ?

   _____

   _____

Giving an Opinion

Which of these implies confidence?

   I believe/think/feel (that) . . .

   I'm convinced (that) . . .

   It seems to me (that) . . .

   _____

   _____

Not Giving an Opinion

Which of these might discourage the conversation from continuing?

I don't feel strongly either way.

Actually I can see both points of view/both sides.

I'm not sure. I haven't really thought about it.

I don't know.

_____

_____

Agreeing

What does it mean if the speaker adds *but* after these phrases?

Right/That's right.

Exactly/That's true.

I think so too, . . .

_____

_____

Hedging

Which of these indicates the most doubt? (try these with different intonations)

    I kind of agree . . .

    I'm pretty much in agreement with you, but . . .

    Probably you're right.

    Well, maybe so, but . . .

    _____

    _____

Disagreeing

Which is a strong statement of disagreement?

    Well, I don't necessarily agree with that.

    Hmmm, I see it somewhat differently.

    I see what you are saying, but . . .

    You're wrong.

    _____

    _____

Exchanging Opinions

Take a look at the following topics. What is your opinion? Why? In this activity you will work in pairs to find out each other's opinions and the reasons for those opinions.

- Get in pairs.
- Spend about 5 minutes discussing the *first* topic (the instructor will tell you when to stop).
- Practice using the phrases from the previous lesson on giving and asking for opinions, as well as the phrases for agreeing, disagreeing, and hedging.
- After instructed to stop, one member of the pair should switch to a new partner and then go on to the *next* topic.
- Hint: Try to take an adversarial role, that is, play the "devil's advocate" once in a while to keep the discussion lively. This strategy is also useful if you both completely agree on a particular topic.

Smoking

Smoking should be banned in all public places.

Smokers have a right to smoke anywhere they like.

Technology

Advances in technology have been a benefit to society.

Advances in technology have caused problems for society.

Language Instruction

Universities should require foreign language study.

Foreign language courses should be optional.

Teaching Assistants

For Undergraduates
There are benefits for undergraduates in having (international) graduate students as teaching assistants.

There are drawbacks for undergraduates in having (international) graduate students as teaching assistants.

For Graduates

There are advantages for international graduate students in being teaching assistants.

There are disadvantages for international graduate students in being teaching assistants.

Add a few current topics that you would like to hear some opinions on.

_____

_____

Questions for Discussions: Getting Started

Take a look at the following article. What do you think about this subject?
If you were in a discussion group, what would you want to say? If you were
leading the discussion, what questions might you ask in order to get your
audience involved in the discussion? Keeping these questions in mind,
complete the following.

State the topic: _____

What *questions* would you ask if you were leading the discussion?

1. _____

2. _____

3. _____

Now, give your own opinion of the topic: _____

_____

Graduate exam joining computer age

■ **Test takers can leave
No. 2 pencils at home by
1996-97 school year.**

FROM THE ASSOCIATED PRESS

NEW YORK – Students taking
the Graduate Record Examination
will soon be able to leave their No. 2
pencils at home.
   The Educational Testing Service
is swapping paper and pencils for
computers, reports in today's edi-
tions of The New York Times and
Washington Post said.
   By the 1996-97 school year, the
400,000 students who annually take
the test – known as the GRE –
will be screened by computer, the
newspapers said.
   The new tests will also be "adap-
tive," meaning that students will
get random questions and, based on
their answers, successive questions
will become harder or easier. Cor-
rectly answering harder questions
will boost scores.
   "This is a huge step in changing
the very nature of testing in the future," said Nancy Cole, president-
elect of the Educational Testing
Service, based in Princeton, N.J. It
administers 9 million tests annually
in the United States and abroad.
   There is no target date for com-
puterizing the SAT, or Scholastic
Aptitude Test, which is taken by 1.8
million high school students for
their college applications.
   Computerized testing, which is
being introduced today for the GRE
on a limited basis, will make test-
taking more convenient and give
students instantaneous results at
the end of the exam. The GRE is
taken by grad school applicants.

From *Ann Arbor News*, November 15, 1993.

More Work on Questions and Discussions

First read the article on the following page.

Do you think that the increase in wages is a good idea or a bad idea? What are the arguments for or against the increase?

_____

_____

_____

What *questions* would you ask if you were leading a discussion on this topic?

1. _____

2. _____

3. _____

Labor Dept. Urged to Reconsider Policy That Raises Pay of Non-U.S. Researchers

WASHINGTON

COLLEGES and universities have urged the U.S. Department of Labor to revise a new policy that forces them to increase the wages they pay to foreign-born researchers.

Labor Department officials say the policy was devised in part to prevent employers from having a financial incentive to hire foreign workers, many of whom may be willing to work for lower wages than U.S. citizens.

The change involves the way that state employment agencies calculate the "prevailing wage" for what are primarily postdoctoral research positions at universities. A large proportion of these positions are filled by foreigners. Previously, agencies surveyed only the universities when determining the wage. Under the new rule, they also must include private companies, which usually pay scientists more than universities pay their postdoctoral researchers.

The modification raised the prevailing wages for such researchers between 30 and 50 per cent, depending on the state, said Cornelius J. Pings, president of the Association of American Universities.

THE CASE OF A JANITOR

The change stems from a ruling by the Labor Department over the hiring of a foreign worker for a janitorial position at a California residential center for emotionally disturbed children. The worker was hired at an hourly wage nearly $5 below the $10.96 standard set by the state employment agency. The residential center argued that its wage was fair because it was the average paid by similar non-profit facilities. However, the Labor Department ruled that, for wage purposes, it could not make distinctions between non-profit and private employers.

The ruling was made a year ago but has begun to affect universities only in recent months, as state employment agencies adjusted the prevailing wages.

"There is nothing to justify separate wages for private and non-profit" employers, a Labor Department official said.

But university officials say that a typical full-time researcher at a university is not the same as a researcher at a private company. Mr. Pings said a university researcher usually means a postdoctoral student. Although such "students" are not working toward a degree, he said, they are "still in the learning process, working under a professor, refining their skills."

Because of the higher salaries, Mr. Pings said, universities have found research much more expensive to carry out. The salaries, he said, have taken a much bigger bite out of the grant funds that support research at universities.

Officials from universities and the associations that represent them have quietly lobbied the Labor Department to change the policy. One solution that has been proposed—and that the Labor Department is seriously considering—is a separate job classification for postdoctoral researchers. "We're really hopeful that they will carve out a title that will have a reliable pool of wages," said a Harvard University spokesman.

Mr. Pings said the Labor Department was aware "that there is a problem here." He also said he was "optimistic" a solution would be found. —AMY MAGARO RUBIN

From *Chronicle of Higher Education*, July 14, 1995.

Now, in your group, do the following.

- Choose a facilitator and have a 3–5 minute discussion on this topic.
- Then, think about the kinds of questions your group thought of. Did your questions keep the discussion going? Did you get everyone's opinion?
- Compare the questions you prepared. Are they the same? Different? Remember, the key to having a successful discussion is having good questions prepared.

As a class, do the following.

- Compare the kinds of questions your group thought of with those from other groups.
- Evaluate these questions. Will they stimulate a good discussion? Why or why not?

Homework

Bring in a short article from a newspaper. The article "Graduate exam joining computer age" on page 52 is an example of the kind you might find for your homework. Remember to include the date and source. Prepare by reading the article and by thinking of questions to get your group's opinions about it. Be ready to summarize the main ideas of your article.

Due on _____

Opinions and Summarizing

It is often difficult to give a concise, short summary of something you have heard or read; nevertheless, it is a useful skill to have. The following activities provide practice in summarizing. You will have a chance to use this skill again in your class discussion.

Read the following article.

- First, underline two or three sentences that you think are important.
- Next, combine these sentences into one or two sentences.
- Then, each of you take a turn and **in your own words** tell the group what the article is about.

The following phrases will be helpful in summarizing the article.

The topic of this article is . . .

The point is that . . .

This article presents information about . . .

Most importantly, . . .

Not surprisingly, . . .

This article focuses on . . .

_____

_____

Ozone-destroyer declining, study says

By PAUL RECER
THE ASSOCIATED PRESS

WASHINGTON — One of the manmade chemicals linked to erosion of the ozone layer around the Earth is decreasing in abundance in the atmosphere, suggesting that an international agreement limiting the chemical is working, researchers reported Friday.

A study published in the journal Science said that measurements taken several times daily since 1978 at five ground monitoring stations around the Earth show about a 2 percent annual decline in methyl chloroform since 1991.

Methyl chloroform is an industrial chemical that is regulated by the 1987 Montreal Protocol, an agreement by most of the world's industrial nations to phase out production and use of chlorofluorocarbons, or CFCs. There are chlorine-based chemicals that are thought to erode the ozone layer.

Researchers said that methyl chloroform is the first of the Montreal Protocol chemicals to show an actual reduction in atmospheric concentration. The other chemicals, which are much more abundant, have stopped increasing, but have not shown an actual decline. The other chemicals also take much longer to break down in the atmosphere than methyl chloroform.

Ozone is a natural barrier against ultraviolet, or UV, radiation from the sun. UV radiation is harmful to many plants and animals and has been shown to cause skin cancer.

The new study was by researchers at Massachusetts Institute of Technology, Scripps Institution of Oceanography, Georgia Institute of Technology in the United States, and at the Commonwealth Scientific and Industrial Research Organization in Australia and the University of Bristol in Britain.

From *Ann Arbor News,* July 15, 1995.

The next article is slightly longer. Read the article, then

- underline at least four sentences or phrases that are important
- combine these sentences into two or three sentences
- **in your own words,** summarize the article

In addition to the phrases on page 56, you might need to use some of the following phrases.

According to Rubin, . . .

North's research shows that . . .

In contrast, Davis stated . . .

However, Davis and others feel that . . .

It is clear that . . .

We can see that . . .

Foreign Influx in Science Found to Cut Americans' Participation

By Amy Magaro Rubin

THE LARGE NUMBER of foreign students enrolling in graduate science and engineering programs in the United States has led universities to become complacent about recruiting Americans, particularly women and members of minority groups, to those fields.

As a result, a new study suggests, stipends paid to graduate students in such programs are lower than they otherwise would be. This lack of financial incentives has further contributed to the decline in American interest in science and engineering programs.

Those are among the main conclusions of a study by David S. North, an independent researcher who has examined immigration issues for 25 years. The findings of the study, which was supported by the Alfred P. Sloan Foundation, have been published by the University Press of America as a book, *Soothing the Establishment: The Impact of Foreign-Born Scientists and Engineers on America*.

Mr. North calls the situation a supply-and-demand issue. Universities have no problem filling slots in science and engineering programs with well-qualified students because of the steady flow of candidates from abroad. Consequently, institutions don't need to "knock themselves out" recruiting and offering higher stipends.

NUMBERS CONTINUE TO GROW

"Since we have such a great supply of foreign-born scientists and engineers at the Ph.D. level, the American establishment is not pressed to change things, to pay more, to recruit more, to get Americans in science and engineering," says Mr. North.

Of the 170,000 graduate students enrolled in U.S. science and engineering programs in academic 1992-93, 43 per cent were from other countries. Of all students who earned graduate degrees in engineering and the sciences from U.S. universities in 1993, 48 per cent were from other countries.

The numbers continue to grow. "No matter how you measure them," Mr. North says, "there are more foreign-born scientists and engineers with each passing year." Universities must start early to reach out to American students to encourage them to pursue graduate training and careers in science and engineering, he says. In addition, stipends should be raised so that Americans will have more of an incentive to enter those fields.

Few officials involved in international education have yet had a chance to read Mr. North's book. However, many are familiar with his conclusions, based on an excerpt that appeared in *Immigration Law Report* in May, and they often disagree.

"Comments like David North's tend to be very one-sided," says Todd M. Davis, director of research at the Institute of Interna-

> **"The establishment is not pressed to change things, to pay more, to recruit more, to get Americans in science and engineering."**

tional Education. "They don't look at the important positives."

The benefits of having international science and engineering students are numerous and wide-ranging, says Mr. Davis. The students are usually the best and the brightest from their countries, thus U.S.

institutions gain from their abilities.

In his study, Mr. North does briefly acknowledge such benefits. He calls the international students a "mixed blessing. They are an attractive group, but they are causing some subtle disruptions."

Some people dispute the suggestion that international students are having a harmful impact.

"I feel he's got the wrong argument," says Fran Helmstadter, who heads the international-scholars office at the Massachusetts Institute of Technology. "There is a problem in getting Americans into these programs, but I don't believe the root of the problem is foreign-born students." She says more Americans would enter science and engineering Ph.D. programs if financial aid were more attractive.

EFFECTS ON LABOR MARKET

Stipends for all graduate students are low, says Peter Syverson, director of research at the Council of Graduate Schools. But he points out that the highest stipends are in science and engineering programs, which also enroll the most international students.

Aside from the impact the international students have on graduate schools, Mr. North suggests that the group affects the American labor market. He says the growth in foreign enrollment has coincided with rising unemployment among young scientists and engineers in the United States. The foreigners, he says, "generally loosened the labor force, leading indirectly to a little more unemployment."

Some question linking the two developments. "When jobs get tight, the old adage is to blame the stranger," says Mr. Syverson. "We have to be careful when we make these comparisons." ∎

From *Chronicle of Higher Education*, July 14, 1995.

More Work on Opinions and Summarizing

Now you will have a chance to work on summarizing and getting opinions about the article you found in the newspaper (homework from p. 55). In your group, do the following.

- First outline below the most important aspects of the topic in three or four sentences or phrases.

    Topic: _____

    Highlights

    a. _____

    b. _____

    c. _____

    d. _____

- Decide who will present first.
- Give a very brief summary of your article; try to do this in one minute (remember, the other members of your group have not seen it).
- Ask someone in your group to paraphrase your summary.
- Check for their understanding of the main issues of your summary.
- Then, use the phrases we have practiced to elicit opinions.
- Take about 3–5 minutes to discuss the issue.

The following phrases might be helpful if you find that the people in your group have not understood what you said.

    That's not quite right . . .

    That's not what I meant.

    You're close, but what I mean is . . .

    _____

    _____

When you have completed each discussion, choose one person to report to the whole class about what went on in their group. Limit these summaries to one minute. Be concise!

These phrases will help with summarizing what happened in your group.

We all agreed that . . .

We discussed the topic . . .

Most of us agree that . . .

After discussing X we all agreed that . . .

_____

_____

Leading a Discussion

- You will each have the opportunity to lead a discussion in class. Your instructor will let you know what the **time limit** is for these discussions. You may lead the discussion with your whole class or with a small group from your class. The following guidelines will be useful in preparing for this longer discussion.
- As the leader, you will need to carefully choose your topic. You should bring in an article or **prepare a handout** for the class. You will need to give this to your group/the class *at least* one class session before your scheduled discussion. This will give everyone a chance to read the article, think about it, and have questions in mind. Discussions are more successful if both the leader and the class are well prepared.
- As the leader, you will need to prepare some **opening remarks** and present some information to give your group/the class the **background** they need. This will set the stage for a successful discussion. You might want to state why this topic was of interest to you. Would a rhetorical question be appropriate? A direct question? The leader might not want to state his/her opinion at this point; it might better fit in later or could be used in the closing. The opening should only be 3–5 minutes, depending on the total time allowed for the discussion. Remember to **check to see if the class is with you**—the discussion will fail if the class/group is lost.
- Prepare some open-ended questions to get the group talking and keep them involved. You might not use all of your prepared questions. **Be flexible.** Remember that it is a good idea to call directly on a classmate, particularly at the beginning of the discussion.
- Finally, you will need to bring the discussion to a comfortable close. When the time allowed is almost up, try to make a **concluding remark**; this might be a summary of what people have expressed, or it might be your own opinion.

Discussion Topics

The first step in leading a discussion is deciding on an appropriate topic for your discussion. There are many sources you can go to if you have no idea of what topic to discuss.

- What are some of the possible *sources* for topics of current interest (e.g., *Time* magazine)?
- What *sources* are there besides books or magazines?
- What *sources* are there in your field of study (journals, etc.)?

Brainstorm with your group about *sources* and list them below. Be specific!

1. _____

2. _____

3. _____

Report to the class about what your group has come up with. Were there any suggestions from other groups that your group hadn't thought of?

After you have looked through different sources and have chosen a topic, you need to decide if it will be an appropriate topic for a discussion. Below are some possible *topics* for discussion. Work with your group to evaluate them. List a positive or negative feature for each topic. If you list a negative feature, see if you can come up with a suggestion for improving the topic or a way to make it workable. Some of the features have been filled in for you as an example.

Topic	Comments	Suggestions for Improvement
The Environment	*too vague, too broad*	*break down into specific area, like mandatory recycling*
The University Treasurer's Report on the End of the Fiscal Year	*too specific, boring, not much info. available*	_____
Smoking in Public Places	_____	_____
Unemployment	_____	*needs more focus; effects of immigration on the economy*
Teachers on Strike	_____	_____
The Influence of TV on Children	_____	*focus on good or bad influences; violence? educational?*
Gays in the Military	*topic applicable only to U.S. situation*	_____
Mandatory English Assessment of International TAs/Students	_____	_____

Organizing the Discussion

Beginning a discussion is often a challenging task. In order to engage your seminar or research group and get them to actively participate, you need to provide a reasonable amount of background on your topic. This will enable the participants to feel comfortable with the topic. Too much information might cause confusion and can reduce the focus of the discussion. The following introduction to a discussion was presented by an international student (A) in a seminar class that consisted of international graduate students and visiting scholars.

Read the following transcript of the introduction to a discussion and then answer the questions that follow.

This transcript was slightly adapted from the original for clarity.
Key to markings on transcript:
    Pauses or silences indicated by . . .

A: [1]Today . . . ah I would like you to discuss with me . . . brain drain of foreign . . . born scientists to the United States . . . and . . . their current marching back to their country. [2]As we know, for several decades ago more than thousand of best student from our country came here for their advanced degree and after they get the degree they still working here. [3]Just most of them don't thinking about going back to work in their country. . . . [4]Uhmm for the article I choose, is the first time I saw, . . . make me very happy because I feel that one day in the future this event will occur . . . in my country. [5]The author of this article say that right now the number of Asian born researcher and scientist . . . uhm who go back, who graduate their degree in United States go back, tend to go back to their hometown, . . . uhm dramatically, the rate is increased dramatically . . . and they say that probably there are several factors influence on this event. [6]For example, the decline of the options for foreigner to get job especially in research field, scientific research field in the United States. [7]And . . . for another reason is the economic boom in their home town, in their homeland. [8]So that might cause them to go back to work in their country. [9]And . . . also just the better offer from Asian institute in universities.

[10]So since all of us are Asian, except C [the instructor] (laughter) I might to know, to present to you from your opinion. [11]Maybe I gonna start with B [Japanese student]. [12]In Japan, scientific and technology in your country . . . do you have a problem about brain drain from Japan to United States or other Western country?

1. What is the topic?

2. Which sentences provide background for the discussion?

3. Where does the speaker offer an opinion?

4. In sentence 2, why does the speaker say "As *we* know . . ." and not "As *I* know . . ."?

5. In sentence 5, the speaker begins with "The author of this article . . ." Why is this important?

6. What is the speaker doing in sentences 6, 7, and 9?

7. In sentence 10, the speaker begins with "So." What is the function of this for the listener?

8. Is the speaker clear about what the focus of the discussion is?

When you introduce the topic of your own discussion, you might use the following phrases. With a partner try to think of a few more ways to express the thought.

To Introduce the Topic

Today I would like to . . .

I want to present . . .

Today I'm going to talk about . . .

_____

_____

To Provide Background

As we know, . . .

As we have already seen, . . .

As we have all read, . . .

For example, . . .

It's clear that . . .

_____

_____

To Focus

Currently, however . . .

More specifically, I would like to discuss . . .

_____

_____

Strategies in Discussions

A successful discussion doesn't just happen; it requires planning and organization on the part of both the leader and the participants. In addition to being well organized, a discussion leader can rely on several different strategies to help the discussion move along. Being aware of and using the following strategies can also help you avoid potential problems in a discussion.

- organizing participation
- follow-up questions
- getting the floor

Read the continuation of the transcript of the discussion and answer the questions that follow.

This transcript was slightly adapted from the original for clarity.
Key to markings on transcript:
     Pauses or silences indicated by . . .

A: [10]So since all of us are Asian, except C [the instructor] (laughter) I might to know, to present to you from your opinion. [11]Maybe I gonna start with B [Japanese student]. [12]In Japan, scientific and technology in your country . . . do you have a problem about brain drain from Japan to United States or other Western country?

B: [13]Actually yes, because as you know Japan is very economical. [14]And in Japan we have big money and big power. [15] . . . But sometime in Japan industry and some university only focus on economy and . . . final product not basic research. [16]So many excellent Japanese scientist want to come to U.S. to do basic research, that very important point about this, I think, about this topic but nowadays in Japan it is just changing. [17]Now we also focus on basic research. [18]We should develop our own opinion about basic research. [19]So I think now changing.

A: [20]Uhh, from your opinion, is it important to focus on basic research?

B: [21]Yes, I think so.

A: [22]Why?

B: [23]Because we used to use . . . American basic research or European basic research but now Japan is . . . one of the top country about research so . . . what you say . . . sometime now we have nothing learn from America or Europe so we want to improve our economy, our technology. [24]We have to develop a new technology by ourselves that's why we have to focus on the basic research.

C: [a Japanese student] [25]I have to add two things, one is the difference . . . between U.S. and Japanese research. [26]In the United States most of research is oriented by . . . university or public research institute but . . . in Japan the most of research is done in company so they only think about benefit of product, so . . . that's why Japanese research, most of Japanese research is not focused on basic research and another thing is . . . educational system in Japan and the United States. [27]In the United States most students is . . . told to be, you know, individual research to seek their idea and apply those idea to new thing, but in Japan it's not. [28]They taught to cooperate with each other . . . to do well in company, not to do a good research.

A: [29]Where is the source of resource in Japan? [30]I mean where do you get the funding for research? [31]What is the source?

C: [32]So when I was in Japan, I did it in company, so company support it.

A: [33]I see, so that why they put more attention on your research that can make a lot of money.

C: [34]And surprisingly in Japanese university, nobody go to Master's course or Ph.D. course for research because they can't get money.

A: [to Korean student "D"] [35]How about the situation about brain drain in Korea? . . . uhm in the present time?

D: [36]In the present time maybe the case is same in Korea as Japan. [37]Usually a Korean company focused on application of technology so they maybe imitate new technology and just try to follow the new . . . state of art technology. [38]So we . . . have no money to invest in basic research and so as . . . our education system focused on many memorizing something and didn't promote the creativity so the problem is educating system. [39]So most of engineer went to United States and come back home. [40]Nowadays, as you told, the trend is changing because of economy boom and they can have many opportunities. [41]So many scientists come back home.

A: [42]Do you think what is the major reason for that scientist and researcher to go back to their home just because economic boom or what?

D: [43]In some sense money, as you told that, money is big cause and if they and work in hometown maybe they have some pride because they can devote their native country they have some opportunity for promotion. [44]If they were in American maybe they is outsider all the time. [45]But in hometown they can some kind of pride and patriotism.

A: [46]OK, . . . uhm as I know China may be the country that have problem in brain drain from your country to the United States. [to Chinese student "E"] [47]Here, I think you probably have more than 1,000 of best students staying here and working making a lot of research and published papers. [48] . . . Why most of Chinese don't, most of them still here, don't think about to go back to work in your country?

E: [49]Briefly, I think it just money . . . (lots of laughter) [50]That's true. [51]I think the situation is very different from this paper, is very different from Japan, Korea, Hong Kong, Taiwan, and Thailand. [52]So because the economy is not so good in China, many people want to do research, oh, no money!

9. What is the strategy "A" uses to get everyone involved in the discussion? (see sentences 11, 35, 46)

10. What is the function of sentences 20, 22, and 42? Are there any other examples?

11. Find where one student joins in the discussion without waiting for the leader's question. How does he begin?

12. For each follow-up question, discuss how the question relates to the previous comments of the participants.

13. Is "A" successful in leading his discussion?

Does he give a good summary of the article?	❑ yes	❑ no
Does he provide appropriate background?	❑ yes	❑ no
Does he keep the discussion focused?	❑ yes	❑ no
Does he get everyone involved?	❑ yes	❑ no
Does he use follow-up questions effectively?	❑ yes	❑ no

To Get the Floor

I have to add two things.

I just want to say . . .

Could I interrupt for a moment . . .

_____

_____

To Encourage Participation

These phrases/questions may be directed to someone in the group who is particularly quiet or who has not yet had the chance to offer an opinion.

So is this situation the same as in *your* country?

Do you agree with what Luis just said?

So, Carolyn, what is *your* opinion of this?

_____

_____

Concluding a Discussion

By being organized and by being familiar with some of the discussion strategies we have considered, you are ready to lead and participate in a successful discussion. But there is one more thing you need to think about and prepare for, and that is how to conclude. In most situations, you will be under a time constraint. In some classes you may be able to stretch your discussion, but, in others, you will have to stop after a certain amount of time no matter whether you are finished or not. So, it is good to have a conclusion prepared, so your audience is not left hanging if you stop abruptly. Your conclusion may be very brief or may include a restatement of your own opinion or perhaps a summary of opinions offered by others.

Look at the following examples of concluding remarks in four different student discussions and then answer the questions that follow.

a. OK, I'm sorry probably we are running out of time so uh let me conclude that uh capital punishment, for capital punishment there are two points of view, and we couldn't decide if should abolish it or not, but the more important thing to prevent crime in society is education as Huang said, and I agree with Huang. OK. Thank you for joining us. Thank you.

b. Yeah, that's all.

c. OK so, um, some of you think that this model is successful, it should not be ignored. So, is Singapore a model for the West? I think this is a big question mark.

d. So we think ah, we, Jen thinks business, government should not be involved too much. The rest of us, I also think so, but ah the rest of us think that government should protect consumer because consumer doesn't know what the airline company is doing.

Answer the following questions with your partner.

1. How are these four examples different?

2. Can you tell what the discussion topic was?

3. Which one do you prefer? Why?

To Conclude

So, to conclude, . . .

In conclusion, . . .

Let me summarize what we've talked about.

We're just about out of time so I'd like to conclude by saying . . .

It looks like our time is up, so . . .

_____

_____

Before the Discussion: A Checklist

❑   Note here some topics you are interested in. If you are stuck, brainstorm with a classmate or check with the instructor for some suggestions.

_____

_____

❑   Confirm the topic with the instructor if you are unsure.

❑   Find an article/prepare handout.

❑   Make enough copies of the handout for the class and distribute them ahead of your scheduled date.

❑   Prepare!

❑   Discuss.

Optional

Fill in the following class schedule. Note who will be the discussion leader and the date. If the class is large, you might be divided into groups. If necessary, note which group you are in.

Discussion Leader	Date	Group
_____	_____	_____
_____	_____	_____
_____	_____	_____
_____	_____	_____
_____	_____	_____
_____	_____	_____
_____	_____	_____
_____	_____	_____

During the Discussion: Feedback

Feedback is a very important part of a discussion. During the upcoming class discussions, you will be participating either as the leader of the discussion or as a member of the group. As the participants in a discussion you will use the same kinds of feedback we discussed in the Active Listening activities of unit 1.

As a member of the group, you might need to ask the leader of the discussion for clarification.

Asking for Clarification

How do you let someone know that you are confused or that you don't know what was just said? Add to the list of phrases that you can use to ask for clarification.

Are you saying that . . .

I don't quite get what you are saying.

Could you repeat that?

_____

_____

_____

As the leader of a discussion you might need to solicit feedback from your audience.

Checking for Understanding

How do you find out if the group is following what you are saying? The
following phrases are useful ways for the discussion leader to get feedback.

Are you following me?

Is that clear?

Is everyone with me?

_____

_____

_____

And, as both the leader of a discussion and as a participant, you might
need to interrupt someone. What are some reasons for interrupting as the
leader? as a participant?

Interrupting

How long do you wait before you interrupt someone? Does this differ from
culture to culture? Add to the list of phrases you can use to interrupt
someone.

Excuse me, but . . .

Ah, I think we need to move on to . . .

Perhaps we can get back to your point after we hear from . . .

_____

_____

_____

During the Discussion: Some Things to Remember

- **Check** to see if students are following your introduction/summary.
- Questions often need to be repeated or restated—**be redundant**—sometimes listeners need to hear questions more than once.
- **Call on** class members by name, especially during the first part of the discussion. It often helps to call the person's name first, then continue with the question—for example: "Takako, do you agree with . . . ?" By doing this you get the person's attention, and they can better focus on the question you will ask.
- **Link comments** from one speaker to the next—for example: "Well, Yuki, what do you think about Jennifer's comment on . . . ?"
- **Paraphrase** some of the comments/opinions, especially if they are very interesting or controversial. This also is a good strategy for clarification.
- Keep the **pace** of the discussion going—give everyone a chance to participate if possible.
- **Interrupt** if needed, especially if you would like to give someone else a chance to speak or comment on a particular point. You could say, "Let's see what Mina has to say about your first point and then if we have time we can come back to you," or, "Excuse me for a moment, but let's hear from someone from Korea, then maybe we can get back to you." You might need to interrupt if one person is dominating the discussion. You may also interrupt to get clarification—for example: "Excuse me, I didn't catch that, could you repeat that before you go on?"
- Keep track of **time** and **conclude.** Sometimes it is hard to stop a lively discussion, but in some situations certain time limits must be followed, so it is good to practice how to end.
- **Avoid over-general questions** (especially at the beginning or end of the discussion)—for example, "Does anyone have any opinion about this article?"
- As participants, be aware of what everyone is saying and respond to them as well as to the leader. **Be an active listener;** pay attention to your nonverbal feedback and body language.

After the Discussion: Feedback

Some written form of feedback is helpful after each discussion, both for the discussion leader and for the participants. As the discussion leader, from the feedback you will get a sense of your own strengths and weaknesses and an idea of what areas need improvement. As participants, you will find that the feedback will help you to evaluate your own participation and help you see for yourselves what you need to work on. By taking time to focus on the discussion immediately after it is over, you will increase your awareness of the roles both the leader and the participants have. This will continue to be of help to you, not only in this class but in other academic courses as well.

It is helpful to receive feedback from your instructor, but it can be equally helpful to receive it from your peers. Making observations about your own participation, a "self-evaluation," is also extremely useful. There are many different types of forms to use for giving feedback, and of course you do not need or want to use all of them all the time. We have provided two examples in appendix 3; one is a self-evaluation form while the other is one your instructor could use to evaluate your discussion. Your instructor might have other versions for you to use, or you might want to come up with your own version. It is not important to use one particular form; what *is* important is to have a chance to think critically about the discussion.

Creating a Feedback Form

Think about how you would evaluate a good discussion. With a partner, list the things you would evaluate in a discussion, the things you feel are important—for example, the leader's eye contact with the class or the clarity of the leader's speech. Keep in mind the kinds of things you would benefit from knowing about your own performance or participation.

Features to Evaluate—Participants   *Features to Evaluate—Leader*

_____   _____

_____   _____

_____   _____

_____   _____

Now, use the above features (all or some) to formulate questions that can become part of a class feedback form.

Follow-up Assignment for Discussions

Part 1

- Choose a topic related to one of the topics we have recently discussed in class (or your instructor may decide that a new topic is appropriate).
- The topic needs to have varying points of view. Prepare a brief introduction of the topic and a summary of your point of view.
- Record your topic and point of view on cassette. Include in your presentation some support for your point of view and then present the listener with three questions that will help you find out his/her point of view.
- The taped presentation and questions should be about 3–5 minutes.
- Speak as clearly as you can so that your classmate will be able to understand your recording.
- Exchange tapes in class.

Due on _____

Part 2

- You will listen to your partner's tape and respond to the questions at the end of the tape.
- You will record your responses after the questions on the tape (or your instructor may have you do this part as a writing assignment instead).
- Respond to all of the questions. You may agree or disagree, fully or partially, but you must give some support for your point of view. In other words, you should not just say, "Oh, yes, I agree," or "I disagree."
- Keep your responses short but informative.

Due on _____

Presenting Data in the Academic Community

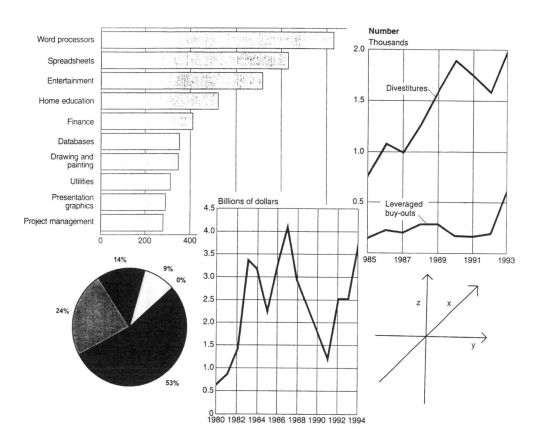

In this unit you will focus on being an expert in discipline-specific discourse. The objective of the activities in this unit is to offer you an opportunity to present, discuss, and exchange discipline-specific information. Many of the activities in this unit are related to nonverbal data in the form of graphs, charts, and tables. These activities give you a chance to practice analyzing, organizing, and synthesizing nonverbal data in order to develop skills needed to present and exchange technical information in an effective and confident style.

Being Explicit: Giving Directions

Being explicit and concise is necessary when presenting data. This will help you give a clear presentation, which in turn will help your audience. Being explicit will also help you keep within designated time limits for presentations, which in some situations may be very strictly enforced.

The next task requires that you work with a partner. One of you will start by describing figure A found in appendix 4, while the other tries to draw it in the space below. Don't let your partner see the drawing while you are describing it. Then you will switch roles and repeat the process using figure B.

Listen to your partner describe figure A or B and try to draw what is being described in the space below.

Being Explicit: Introducing the Task

1. How did your partner begin his/her description?

2. What other ways might you begin your description of these shapes?

    Here are some examples of how other students began their descriptions of different designs.

    a. "There is a circle in the left side of the square, with the side of the square as its diameter. Under the square there is a right triangle. Its right angle is connected with the square."

    b. "How to describe? A wavy line is on the left side of the paper. An equilateral triangle . . ."

    c. "I'd like you to draw the picture I have invented and I will explain all the directions as clear as it is possible for me. Step one, draw a . . ."

    d. "Now we begin our greatest piece of art. Now please draw a triangle, a big triangle in the upper side of your paper because we have to draw another shape under the triangle. So draw the big triangle on the upper side. Then draw a circle in your triangle. The circle touches each side of your triangle. You must notice that each side did touch the circle."

3. How are the above introductions different? Which, if any, do you prefer?

4. Describe how the following examples help the listener.

    e. "This is (name). Relax yourself. Are you ready? OK let's go. First you draw a square in the middle of the paper. Next . . ."

    f. "Hello. It's my pleasure to do the following exercise with you. Are you ready? There are six steps to finish your drawing. Let's begin step by step. Step one, draw a square."

5. How do these examples help you prepare to begin a discussion or present information to a group of students or colleagues?

Being Explicit: Homework

Part 1

Choose some shapes, lines, and figures and use them to draw your own design below or on a separate piece of paper. You may use these shapes and lines in any combination you wish. Then, tape-record your description of your design. One of your classmates will have to draw the design by listening to your description. Bring the tape and the drawing to the next class. Exchange tapes with a classmate. Give your drawing to the instructor.

Due on _____
Name: _____

Part 2

Listen to your partner's tape and draw his/her design according to what you hear. Draw the design here or on a separate piece of paper. Give your partner some feedback on his/her instructions.

Due on _____

Name: _____

Instructions by _____

Comment on the instructions. Were they easy, clear, complicated, organized, confusing, difficult to follow, fun, challenging, etc.?

_____

_____

Technical Vocabulary

Having the appropriate technical vocabulary to describe figures and data is another necessary component of giving clear presentations. Some technical vocabulary is very field specific and idiosyncratic; some is rapidly changing or being newly created to keep up with advances in technology, particularly in computer related fields. These next activities will introduce you to and give you practice with the basic technical vocabulary used to describe illustrations, figures, and technical objects. Work with a partner to answer the questions about the following figures.

Describe the relationship of the lines in each of the following figures/diagrams.

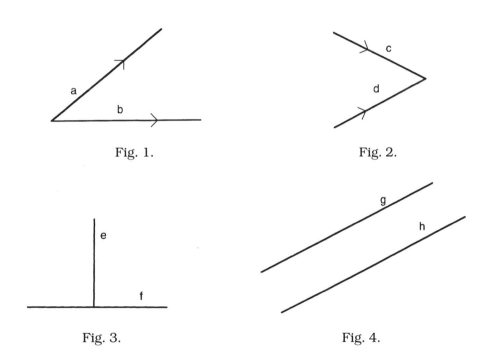

Fig. 1.　　　　　　　　　　　　　　　Fig. 2.

Fig. 3.　　　　　　　　　　　　　　　Fig. 4.

Identify the angles shown in the following figures.

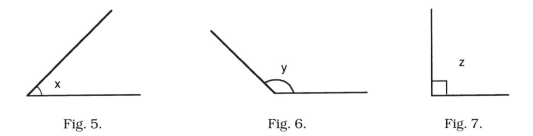

Fig. 5.　　　　　　　　Fig. 6.　　　　　　　　Fig. 7.

Identify the directions of lines x, y, and z in the following diagram.

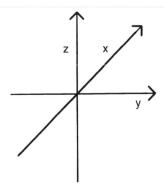

Fig. 8.

Describe the location of the star in each figure. Be explicit.

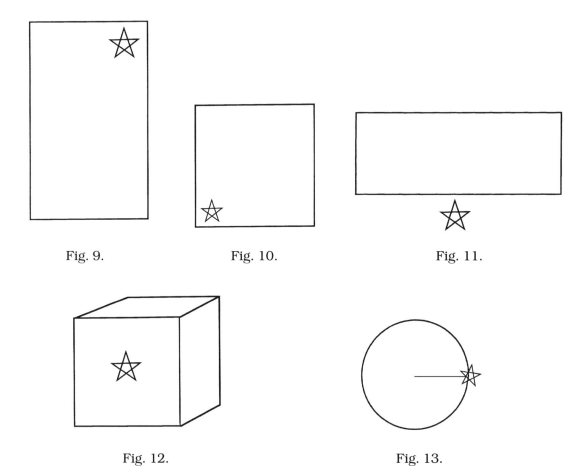

Fig. 9.   Fig. 10.   Fig. 11.

Fig. 12.   Fig. 13.

Describe where the opening is in each figure. Be explicit.

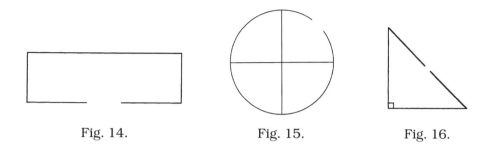

Fig. 14.   Fig. 15.   Fig. 16.

Match the terms on the left with the figures on the right.

adjacent   Fig. 17.

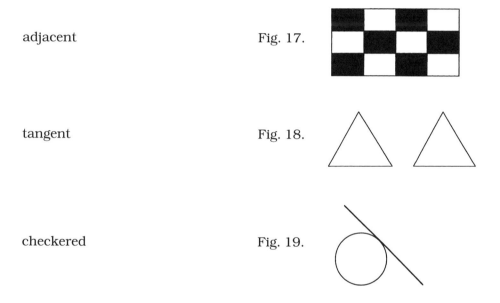

tangent   Fig. 18.

checkered   Fig. 19.

Estimate the distances and sizes of the following figures using the scale given below.

Scale: |————————————————|
                  5 cm

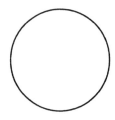

Fig. 20.

Fig. 20 is approximately ————————— cm in diameter.

Fig. 21.   Fig. 21 is approximately ————————— cm deep.

Fig. 22.   Fig. 22 is approximately ————————— cm high.

Describe the following figures.

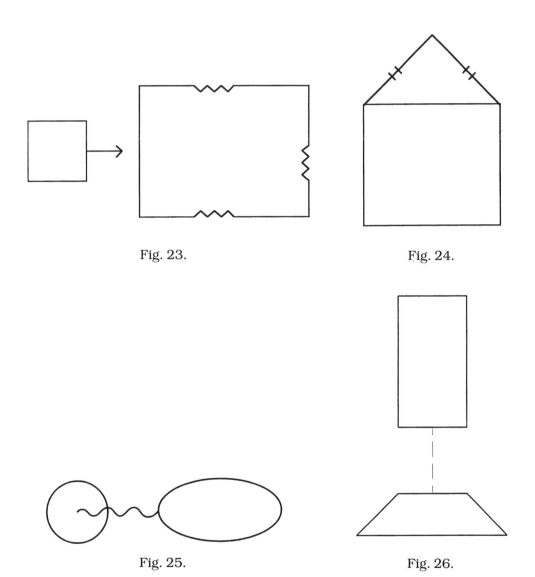

Fig. 23.

Fig. 24.

Fig. 25.

Fig. 26.

Idioms from Geometry

Some common idiomatic expressions are drawn from mathematics and geometry. If you are familiar with the language of mathematics, you may be able to guess the meaning of these expressions.

Work with a partner and try to come up with the meaning for the idiomatic expressions given below. The expressions are italicized.

I asked him to *give me a straight answer,* but he just kept *going around in circles.*

I thought I remembered the author of the book, but when the professor asked me I just *drew a blank.*

When I was giving my presentation the professor asked me to *get to the point* because we were running out of time. I guess I had *gone off on a tangent.*

To understand what this essay means you need *to read between the lines.*

Could you explain this to me again and *start at square one.*

One way to make your example clearer would be *to draw a parallel* between the two writers.

An Introduction to Nonverbal Data: Graphs, Charts, Tables

In many cases, when you have to give a presentation or discuss your research with your peers or colleagues, you will have to refer to some visual information—for example, graphs, charts, or figures. The following activities will introduce you to the terminology you will need to do this.

Graphs

Graphs are diagrams that usually represent the relationship between variables, shown on the vertical, or *y*, axis and the horizontal, or *x*, axis.

1. What is the general term for this kind of graph?

2. What time span is covered?

3. What does the vertical axis represent?

   the horizontal axis?

4. What are the revenues measured in?

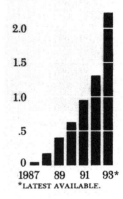

Blockbuster

The firm's revenues have soared, largely because of expansion.

By year

IN BILLIONS OF DOLLARS

5. What is the general term for this kind of graph?

6. What division ranked highest? lowest?

7. What are the revenues measured in?

By division

IN MILLIONS OF DOLLARS

Film $225

Music $405

Video $1,597

Total $2.23 billion

SOURCE: BLOCKBUSTER

From *Newsweek*, February 20, 1995 (source: Blockbuster).

Figure 22.2
Consumer Complaints Against
U.S. Airlines: 1986 to 1994

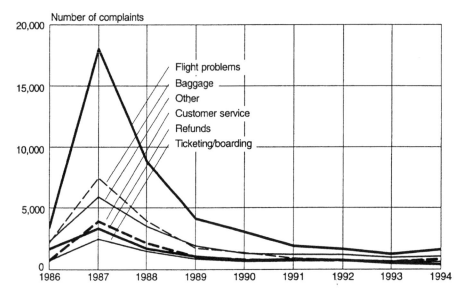

Source: Chart prepared by U.S. Bureau of the Census. For data, see table 1070.

From U.S. Bureau of the Census (Washington, D.C.: U.S. GPO, 1995).

8.   What is the general term for this kind of graph?

9.   What does the horizontal axis represent? the vertical axis?

Use the following phrases to describe the activity represented by this graph. There may be several possible ways to use these phrases.

10.   sharp decrease

11.   gradual increase

12.   steady decrease

13.   levels off

14.   parallels

Charts

A flowchart or an organizational chart uses a combination of words and graphics to visually represent organization or structure. Usually the relationship between parts of the chart is indicated by arrows on the chart, which may "flow" in one or more directions.

Here is an example from the hotel industry.

Exhibit 3.2   Guest-Front Office Interaction During the Guest Cycle

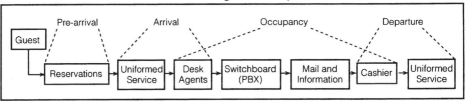

From *Managing Front Office Operations* (Educational Institute of the American Hotel & Motel Association: 1988)

1.   What are the four stages of the guest cycle?

2.   What occurs during the occupancy stage?

3.   What do the broken lines indicate?

4.   How would you summarize the guest cycle?

Tables

Tables are another way to visually represent data. Data is arranged in vertical columns and horizontal rows. Often the same data could be represented in a table or in a graph. How do tables differ from graphs? Which one focuses on summarizing the data?

The following three tables are from the *American Journal of Economics and Sociology.* The article gives an analysis of contributors to the journal. It describes who wrote articles for the journal and what institutions were represented during the years 1991–93.

Table 1
CONTRIBUTIONS BY TYPES OF INSTITUTION

Institutions	Number of Institutions	%	Number of Pages	%	Number of Papers	%
U.S. Academic	225	75.50	5086.83	80.59	443.33	79.45
Foreign[a]	49	16.44	941.83	14.92	85.17	15.26
U.S. Private	17	5.71	172.34	2.73	21.00	3.76
U.S. Gov't	5	1.68	93.00	1.47	7.00	1.26
Others[b]	2	0.67	18.00	0.29	1.50	0.27
Totals	298	100	6312	100	558	100

[a]'Foreign' contains academic, government, and private foreign institutions.
[b]Unaffiliated authors are counted as others.

Table 2
CONTRIBUTIONS FROM FOREIGN INSTITUTIONS

Rank	Country	Papers	%	Pages	%	Institutions	Authors
1	Canada	24.00	28.18	275.00	29.20	11	14
2	Australia	13.50	15.85	158.00	16.78	6	8
3	Germany	12.25	14.38	114.75	12.18	3	3
4	Netherlands	8.00	9.40	105.00	11.15	4	4
5	New Zealand	8.00	9.40	72.00	7.65	4	7
6	England	6.00	7.05	44.00	4.67	7	7
7	Taiwan	2.67	3.14	32.00	3.40	2	2
8	Israel	2.50	2.94	30.33	3.22	3	4
9	Thailand	1.00	1.17	15.00	1.59	1	1
10	Ireland	1.00	1.17	14.00	1.49	1	1
	Mexico	1.00	1.17	14.00	1.49	1	1
12	Nigeria	1.00	1.17	12.00	1.27	1	1
	India	1.00	1.17	12.00	1.27	1	1
14	Jamaica	1.00	1.17	11.00	1.17	1	1
	Singapore	1.00	1.17	11.00	1.17	1	1
16	Switzerland	0.75	0.88	11.25	1.19	1	1
17	Norway	0.50	0.59	10.50	1.11	1	1
	Totals	85.17	100	941.83	100	49	58

Table 3
CONTRIBUTIONS BY ACADEMIC DISCIPLINE OF AUTHORS

Rank	Discipline	Papers	%	Pages	%	Authors	%
1	Economics	308.69	55.32	3513.16	55.66	247	56.52
2	Pol Science	46.83	8.39	561.67	8.90	30	6.86
3	Business	45.81	8.21	514.40	8.15	43	9.84
4	Sociology	44.25	7.93	518.00	8.21	41	9.38
5	Urban & Reg	19.50	3.49	241.34	3.82	14	3.20
6	Geography	13.50	2.42	141.50	2.24	6	1.37
7	Law	13.50	2.42	131.00	2.08	5	1.14
8	Philosophy	9.00	1.61	98.50	1.56	5	1.14
9	History	8.00	1.43	110.00	1.74	7	1.60
10	Religion	3.50	0.62	39.50	0.63	2	0.46
11	Education	3.00	0.54	40.00	0.63	1	0.23
12	Medicine	3.00	0.54	24.00	0.38	1	0.23
13	Environmental	2.67	0.48	32.67	0.52	3	0.69
14	English	2.00	0.36	29.00	0.46	2	0.46
15	Journalism	2.00	0.36	20.00	0.32	3	0.69
16	Natural Science	2.00	0.36	19.00	0.30	4	0.92
17	Anthropology	0.59	0.11	9.66	0.15	1	0.23
18	Engineering	0.50	0.09	7.00	0.11	1	0.23
19	Native Studies	0.50	0.09	6.50	0.10	1	0.23
20	Architecture	0.33	0.06	5.00	0.08	1	0.23
21	Others	28.83	5.17	250.00	3.96	19	4.35
	Totals	558	100	6312	100	437	100

1. Give a summarizing statement for Table 1.

2. How does Table 2 relate to Table 1?

3. Summarize Table 2.

4. Keeping in mind that this particular journal is an interdisciplinary one, what summarizing statement could you make about Table 3?

Homework

Bring to class a graph, chart, or table from your own field of study. Make an extra copy to hand in. Remember to note the reference. You will use this graph in a small group activity. You should think about the following things before class.

- introduction (situation, problem, motivate interest)—why is this relevant to your field?
- highlights of the data (not all the details)
- summary statement about what the graph tells you

Summarizing Nonverbal Data

Work with a partner to complete the following questions about this line graph.

1. What is the subject of the graph?

2. How would you summarize the changes between 1975 and 1980? Between 1980 and 1990?

3. Which product exhibits a steady growth pattern?

4. How can you describe steel cans in relation to the overall production of beverage cans?

5. What predictions can you make? What trends will most likely continue?

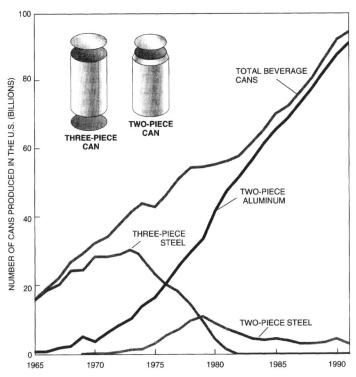

ANNUAL BEVERAGE CAN PRODUCTION in the U.S. has increased by several billion over the past few years. The two-piece aluminum can overwhelmingly dominates the market; steel cans constitute less than 1 percent. Three-piece steel cans, which are now rarely made, reached their peak production in the mid-1970s.

From William F. Hosford and John L. Duncan, "The Aluminum Beverage Can," *Scientific American,* September 1994. Copyright ©1994 by Scientific American, Inc. All rights reserved.

Take a look at these three graphs about fertility rates around the world. As you can see, the horizontal axis represents the average number of children a woman produces, and this is the same on all three graphs.

1. Write a summarizing statement for the second graph.

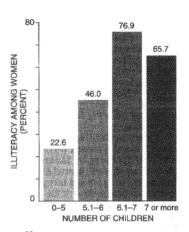

2. Write a summarizing statement for the third graph.

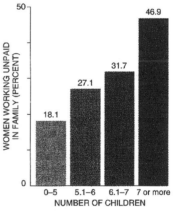

3. Now look at the first graph. What connection does this graph have with the other two? Write a statement showing the relationship between the three graphs.

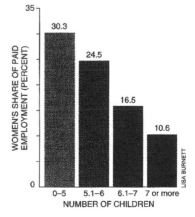

From Partha S. Dasgupta, "Population, Poverty and the Local Environment," *Scientific American*, February 1995. Copyright ©1995 by Scientific American, Inc. All rights reserved.

In the academic community, when you present or write up your own research, you will need to make decisions as to how to represent your data. Which type of nonverbal representation will you choose? Think about the differences and similarities between the different kinds of nonverbal data representations we have been looking at.

Following is an example of representing the same nonverbal data in two different ways.

1. What do you focus on in the bar graph in Figure 1? What do you immediately notice?

2. What does Table 3 show you that the graph doesn't?

3. Why use both? How do these two things function in the article?

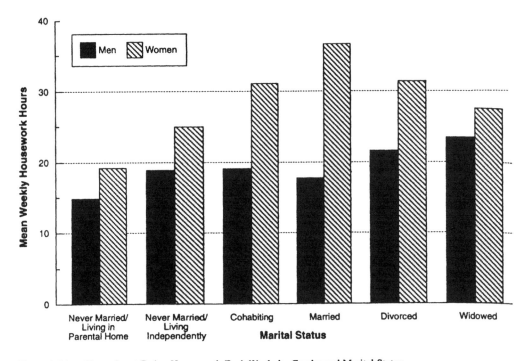

Figure 1. Mean Hours Spent Doing Housework Each Week, by Gender and Marital Status

From *American Journal of Economics and Sociology*, October 1993.

Table 3. Mean Hours Spent per Week in Various Household Tasks, by Marital Status and Gender: U.S. Men and Women, 1987 to 1988

Household Task[b]	Marital Status[a]					
	Never Married/ Living in Parental Home	Never Married/ Living Independently	Cohabiting	Married	Divorced	Widowed
Women						
Preparing meals	3.64	6.74	7.99	10.14	8.15	7.96
Washing dishes	3.92	4.38	5.51	6.11	5.14	4.73
Cleaning house	3.95	5.16	7.10	8.31	6.68	5.68
Washing/ironing	2.45	2.63	3.44	4.16	3.37	2.50
Outdoor maintenance	1.39	1.24	1.34	2.06	1.94	2.26
Shopping	1.72	2.28	2.69	2.86	2.67	2.40ns
Paying bills	.81ns	1.53	1.66	1.52	1.70	1.48ns
Car maintenance	.48	.42	.28	.16	.40	.20
Driving	.90ns	.65	1.10ns	1.34	1.30	.38ns
Total housework hours	19.26	25.04	31.12	36.67	31.37	27.59
Number of cases	383	649	248	3,838	829	817
Men						
Preparing meals	2.23	5.06	3.71	2.69	5.50	6.48
Washing dishes	1.92	2.77	2.63	2.15	3.24	3.87
Cleaning house	2.20	2.97	2.60	2.03	3.54	3.38
Washing/ironing	1.30	1.92	1.16	.70	1.75	1.67
Outdoor maintenance	3.56	1.56	3.18	4.94	2.60	3.38
Shopping	.83	1.92	1.73	1.58	1.93	2.14ns
Paying bills	.90ns	1.38	1.35	1.32	1.45	1.65ns
Car maintenance	1.23	.92	1.51	1.37	.99	.52
Driving	.75ns	.42	1.28ns	1.04	.57	.41ns
Total housework hours	14.93	18.92	19.16	17.83	21.56	23.49
Number of cases	477	476	181	2,668	323	127

[a] All associations between marital status and time spent on household tasks are significant at the $p < .05$ level.

[b] Within marital status and task type, all gender differences are significant at the $p < .05$ level with the following exceptions (marked ns): for never married in parental home--paying bills and driving; for cohabitor--driving; for widows--shopping, paying bills, and driving.

Presenting the Data 1

Take a look at the graphs you brought to class from your own field of study (homework from p. 99).

You should take about 3–5 minutes to present your graph to each other/to the group. Remember to include the following information.

- introduction (situation, problem, motivate interest)
- why this is relevant to your field
- highlights of the data (not all the details)
- summary statement about what the graph tells you

As the listener, remember to ask for clarification if information is not clear or not given.

Difficult Questions: Asking and Answering

Answering Questions

You often open the floor to questions after presenting a paper on your own research. Or, you will have to field questions during the course of a discussion. Whatever the context, you might find yourself in the position of not being able to answer someone's question. There may be a couple of reasons for this. It is possible that the way the question is being asked is just not clear, or perhaps you do not know the answer to the question. For whatever reason it happens that you cannot answer a question, there are strategies you can use to help you get out of a difficult situation.

Asking Questions

As a member of an audience, you will often have the opportunity to ask questions about a presentation after it is finished. You need to be aware of your interaction with the speaker when asking questions. If your question is not being answered, it is possible that you are not asking a clear and direct question or that the speaker does not know the answer. There are strategies you can use in this situation that can make the interaction between you and the speaker less awkward.

Strategies for answering

- Reword or paraphrase the question being asked. This gives you some extra time and might solve the problem.
- If you still can't understand or follow the question, you can ask for clarification.
- If that fails, you can try to gracefully redirect the question to an area you are familiar with.
- Offer to "talk later."

Strategies for asking

- Reword your question if you are not being understood.
- Be direct.
- Know when to stop.

Keep this list of strategies in mind when working on the next activity.

The following is an example of a question-answer interaction, taken from the end of a student's presentation of data. Read the following transcript and answer the questions that follow. The speaker (A) was presenting an economics graph titled "Index of Consumer Sentiment and Car Sales" and asked if there were any questions. A classmate in the audience (B) had a question.

A simplified version of the graph is given to help you visualize what the students are talking about. The right vertical axis represents the index of consumer sentiment. The left vertical axis represents the number of car sales, in millions. The horizontal axis represents years, from 1968 through 1982. The thick line represents car sales; the thin line represents the index.

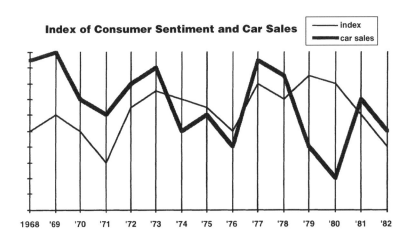

This transcript was slightly adapted from the original for clarity.
Key to markings on transcript:
    Pauses or silences indicated by . . .
    Overlap of speakers indicated by vertical line
    Unintelligible speech indicated by [---]

[1]*A:* Thank you. Are there any questions?

[2]*B:* . . . please explain why there is a lag between these two lines?

[3]*A:* Between these two lines is a what?

[4]*B:* lag . . . L-A-G . . . lag . . . because it's a time [---] we will have a

    lag, I think so . . . uh I would like to . . . these two line have a

    difference

[5]*A:*   Oh yeah there is some difference

[6]*B:* Why? . . . Why there have some distance?

[7]*A:* Because the index of consumer sentiment is a predictor . . . uh

the car sales is a . . . is a real . . . is from a real data . . . the car sales

. . . there is no difference

[8]*B:* so index must be leading . . . compared with the index but car sales

seems to be leading . . . compared with the index, right? . . . don't you

think so?

[9]*A:* I'm sorry I I . . . I can't understand your question

[10]*B:* um, yeah, clearly car sales is a lag   a lag

[11]*A:*   is a lag? . . . oh it's a lag

[12]*B:* and after that index is moving, right? . . . why?

[13]*A:*   uh . . . we [---] the index first

[14]*B:* but car sales moves first, right? . . . for example 73 . . . between 73 74

and 1978 and what, what is that I don't . . . I don't see well . . . car

sales moves first

[15]*A:* oh you mean the car sales move first

[16]*B:* right . . . after that index . . . goes upwards

[17]*A:* oh I see . . . [long pause] . . . uh . . . I don't think there's a car sales

move first

[18]*B:*   isn't it?

[19]*A:* This is a . . . this means car sales are more than the index . . . more

than the index . . . the I mean uh [pause, laughter] the car sales are

larger than the index

[20]*B:* in what respect?

[21]*A:* uh the car sales . . . um the car sales are more than the consumer [---]

[22]*B:* ok good you change here car sales are the leading

[23]*A:*   huh   oh *no* it's *not*

leading . . . the index is from . . . um . . . the responders answer
but the car sales is from the real data

[24]*B:*   so what is this index for?

[25]*A:*   you mean the index for?

[26]*B:*   look backwards index?

[27]*A:*   oh, the index is for future

[28]*B:*   for future . . . but it lag?

Questions

1.   What strategy does "A" use in lines 3 and 9? Are they helpful to the discussion? Do they move the discussion ahead?

2.   The speaker starts to paraphrase by saying "oh you mean" in line 15. Is she successful in her paraphrase?

3.   How many times does "B" ask a question?

4.   What advice would you give "B"?

5.   What could you have done if you were "A" in this situation?

You might use some of these phrases when you are presenting data. Can you add any to the list?

To Paraphrase or Reword Questions

In other words, . . .

What I'm saying is . . .

I mean, . . .

_____

_____

To Ask for Clarification

What do you mean?

I'm sorry, what exactly is your question?

I guess I just don't see your point. Could you clarify?

_____

_____

To Redirect the Question

That's a very interesting question. What I *have* looked at is . . .

That's a good question, but in my case . . .

I don't have the data (yet), but . . .

That's our next step.

_____

_____

To Postpone

We haven't thought much about that yet, but if you'd like to talk afterward we can.

I'd like to hear more about what you are saying.

I feel I've answered the question, but we could continue our discussion later.

_____

_____

Rewording Questions

In this activity you will have a chance to practice rewording questions. There are a few simple guidelines for rewording questions.

- Be concise.
- Stay on the same topic; that is, don't ask a *different* question.
- Use synonyms.
- Try different grammatical forms.

For example

Original question: What do the two lines on the graph indicate?

Rewording: What is the difference between the two lines on the graph?

Rewording: Please explain why there is a lag between those two lines.

Now, come up with two of your own questions. Pretend that you are asking a question after a colleague's presentation (any topic will do). Write them below, then have your partner reword your question.

1. your question:_____

_____

rewording:_____

_____

rewording:_____

_____

2. your question:_____

_____

rewording:_____

_____

rewording:_____

_____

Presenting the Data 2

You will have a chance to give a short presentation of some nonverbal data (a chart, graph, table, etc.) specific to your own field of study. You will need to have the illustration reproduced on an overhead or as a handout or drawn on the board. Remember that your audience will be trying to complete the "Audience Questionnaire" on page 113 while they are listening to your presentation. Keep these questions in mind. You can use these questions to help you organize your presentation. You should also try to do the following things.

- Remember who your audience is—who they are and what their level of expertise in your field is.
- Check for audience understanding early in the presentation.
- Watch your timing (practice ahead of time) and allow a minute for questions/comments.
- Ask for questions.

Schedule for Presentations

Date   Name

_____   _____

_____   _____

_____   _____

_____   _____

_____   _____

_____   _____

Audience Questionnaire for Data Presentations

Fill out the following form after the presentation. If you did not get enough information or the information wasn't clear, ask a question of the presenter.

1. Presenter's name   His/her field of study

2. What is the importance of the graph/chart/design to this field?

3. What are the variables (or, important components, measurements, characteristics)?

4. What are the significant outcomes?

5. What can you conclude (i.e., make a statement summarizing the main point of the illustration)?

[this page may be reproduced as needed]

Follow-up Assignment on Presenting Data

Homework

- Attach a copy of a graph, chart, table, etc., from your own field of study.
- Write a short introductory statement.
- List highlights.
- Summarize.

Introduction

_____

_____

_____

Highlights

_____

_____

_____

Summary

_____

_____

_____

Formal Introductions

Interacting, participating, presenting . . . for some of you these may be things you will do almost every day in your life in the academic community. For others these will come together in the context of the professional conference.

At professional conferences, speakers are often introduced by a colleague. The introduction includes a certain standard set of information. List the kind of information you would need to know about someone in order to introduce him/her at a conference.

_____

_____

_____

_____

_____

_____

Here is an example of a formal introduction.

> It gives me great pleasure to introduce John Swales, Director of the English Language Institute and Professor of Linguistics at the University of Michigan. Professor Swales is the author of numerous articles and books on English for Specific Purposes, including his most recent, _Genre Analysis._ In addition, he has most recently coauthored an EAP writing text with Christine Feak entitled _Academic Writing for Graduate Students._ Today he will speak on the topic of tasks and discipline-specific texts for international graduate students. Let's welcome John Swales.

1. What are some other ways to start an introduction?

2. Who might the audience be for such an introduction?

3. Sometimes a formal introduction will include a personal anecdote, the speaker's educational background or previous employment, or something humorous. At what point in the introduction would you mention these things?

Look at the following introduction.

> Today, we are going to hear from Sarah, my friend and colleague at the ELI. Sarah Briggs has her Ph.D. She is the Associate Director of Testing. She has two children. She writes some interesting articles and gives presentations on testing international teaching assistants. I hope we enjoy listening to Ms. Briggs since she is an expert in interviewing and listening tasks in test situations.

4. Is it formal enough for an introduction at a conference? Are there other problems with it? Provide some suggestions to improve the introduction.

Now interview a partner in class and find out as much information as you need to introduce him/her at a conference.

Notes

Prepare your introduction and be ready to introduce your partner on the last day of class.

Appendixes

Question Sets A and B for "Getting to Know You"

Getting to Know You—Questions for GROUP A

Write your answers to these questions in the appropriate places on the diagram on page 5.

1. When did you first leave your country?

2. Name the most beautiful place in the world you have visited.

3. What language(s) do you speak?

In the circle under number 3: How long have you been in the United States?

In the circle above number 4: Write the name of your spouse.

4. What department (or school/field of study) will you be in?

5. What university or school did you attend before coming here?

6. How many people are in your immediate family, including yourself?

In the top right square: Put the city and country you are from.

In the bottom left square: Have you been to the university library?

In the middle square: Print the name you prefer to be called in class.

Around the square: List three things you enjoy doing.

Getting to Know You—Questions for GROUP B

Write your answers to these questions in the appropriate places on the diagram on page 5.

1. Have you visited any other states in the United States? If so, what states?

2. Name the most beautiful place in the world you have visited.

3. What language(s) do you speak?

In the circle under number 3: When did you arrive here?

In the circle above number 4: Are you married or single?

4. What department (or school/field of study) will you be in?

5. What university or school did you attend before coming here?

6. What's the population of your country?

In the top right square: Name the leader of your country.

In the bottom left square: Have you been to the university library?

In the middle square: Print the name you prefer to be called in class.

Around the square: List three things you dislike doing.

Instructions for the Designated Interrupter

The following instructions will be assigned to the Designated Interrupter by the instructor. (Cut on dotted lines.)

- - ✂ -

> Interrupter A: After 30 seconds (or a few seconds into the presentation) you will attempt to interrupt and get the speaker's opinion about the topic of discussion. Try to do this at least two times.

- - ✂ -

> Interrupter B: Interrupt the speaker with a question totally unrelated to the topic. Try to do this at least two times.

- - ✂ -

> Interrupter C: Interrupt the presenter with a question showing that you are unsure of something she/he is saying. If your question is answered and you are sure of the meaning, give the appropriate feedback. If not, ask again.

- - ✂ -

[this page may be reproduced as needed]

Feedback Forms for Discussions

Discussion Self-Evaluation

Name: _____

Write in the topics of the past three discussions and comment on the topic choices.

Topic: _____
comments

Topic: _____
comments

Topic: _____
comments

Evaluate *yourself* as a participant in the past three discussions. Have you improved in the areas you wrote down on the last evaluation?

As a participant in the next three discussions, what will you try to work on/improve?

[this page may be reproduced as needed]

Instructor's Evaluation Form for Discussions

Name of Discussion Leader:

Date:

Topic:

Note strengths and weaknesses in the following areas:

Preparation
    Topic choice appropriate
    Handouts ready ahead of time
    Enough questions prepared

Introduction
    Summary of topic

Discussion
    questions
    follow-ups
    involved all/most of class
    kept discussion moving
    interrupted
    paraphrased

Conclusion
    brought topic to close

Timing

Language

Other

[this page may be reproduced as needed]

Figures A and B for "Being Explicit: Giving Directions"

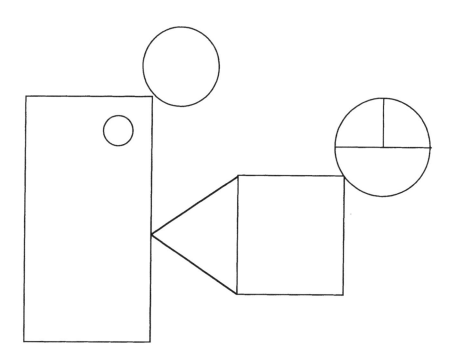

Fig. A

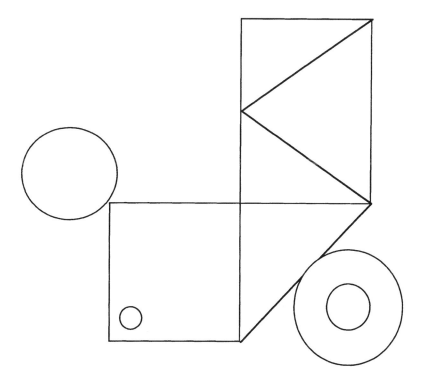

Fig. B

References

Bardovi-Harlig, K., and B. S. Hartford. 1993. Learning the rules of academic talk. *Studies in Second Language Acquisition* 15:279–304.

Boxer, D., and L. Pickering. 1995. Problems in the presentation of speech acts in ELT materials: The case of complaints. *ELT Journal* 49, no. 1:44–58.

Chips off the block. 1995. *Newsweek,* February 20.

Dasgupta, P. S. 1995. Population, poverty and the local environment. *Scientific American,* February, 40–45.

Hirokawa, K. 1995. *Expressions of Culture in Conversational Styles of Japanese and Americans.* Ph.D. diss., University of Michigan, Ann Arbor.

Hosford, W. F., and J. L. Duncan. 1994. The aluminum beverage can. *Scientific American,* September, 48–53.

McChesney, B. J. 1994. The functional language of the U.S. TA during office hours. In *Discourse and Performance of International Teaching Assistants,* edited by C. G. Madden and C. L. Myers, 134–52. Alexandria, VA: Teachers of English to Speakers of Other Languages (TESOL).

Mehdizadeh, M. 1993. An analysis of authors and institutions contributing to the AJES, 1981–93. *American Journal of Economics and Sociology* 52, no. 4:459–66.

U.S. Bureau of the Census. 1995. *Statistical Abstracts of the United States: 1995.* Washington, D.C.: U.S. GPO.